Sweden

Sweden

BY ANN HEINRICHS

Enchantment of the World™
Second Series

CHILDREN'S PRESS®

An Imprint of Scholastic Inc.

New York   Toronto   London   Auckland   Sydney
Mexico City   New Delhi   Hong Kong
Danbury, Connecticut

Frontispiece: **Riddarholm Church, Stockholm**

Consultant: Susan Brantly, PhD, Professor, Department of Scandinavian Studies, University of Wisconsin–Madison

Please note: All statistics are as up-to-date as possible at the time of publication.

Book production by The Design Lab

Library of Congress Cataloging-in-Publication Data
Heinrichs, Ann.
 Sweden / by Ann Heinrichs.
 pages cm. — (Enchantment of the world, second series)
 Includes bibliographical references and index.
 ISBN 978-0-531-22017-7 (lib. bdg.)
 1. Sweden—Juvenile literature. I. Title.
 DL609.H45 2014
 948.5—dc23   2013022562

1 2 3 4 5 6 7 8 9 10 R 23 22 21 20 19 18 17 16 15 14

Girl in the snow

Contents

Left to right: **Stockholm, rural church, moose, Sámi and reindeer, logging truck**

CHAPTER 1

A Land of Tradition

SIGRID LEAVES SCHOOL AT 3:15 P.M. HER BOOTS make a crunchy sound as she crosses the frosty schoolyard. It's Friday, and she's looking forward to a nice evening at home. She fastens her bike helmet, flips her bicycle headlight on, and starts her ten-minute ride. Darkness is already descending on this chilly winter's day in Sweden. Sigrid's headlight brightens her way along the gloomy bike path.

At home, Pappa helps Sigrid peel off her outer layers of warm clothes. Mamma is still at work, and Pappa is taking care of Sigrid's baby brother, Viggo. In Sweden, fathers can take time off from work to care for their children.

After Mamma gets home, she helps Sigrid design her crown for Lucia Day. This December holiday is a big event nationwide. It's a blend of old traditions, popular culture, and legends of Saint Lucia, a Christian holy woman. Many schools and towns select a girl as Lucia, and Sigrid's school chose her this year. She will lead a candlelight procession wearing a traditional crown of

Opposite: **In Sweden, bicycling is an everyday way of getting around. It is estimated that two-thirds of Swedes are cyclists.**

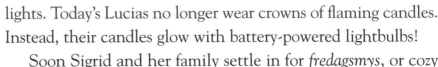

lights. Today's Lucias no longer wear crowns of flaming candles. Instead, their candles glow with battery-powered lightbulbs!

Soon Sigrid and her family settle in for *fredagsmys*, or cozy Friday. They put on comfy clothes, curl up on the couch with pizza and snacks, and watch old movies on TV. It's the perfect way to end the week with some family time.

People have been telling tales of the Vikings' brave voyages for more than a thousand years.

Traces of Culture

This snapshot of Sigrid's life reveals much about Sweden's culture. Consider her name and her brother's, for example. Both Sigrid and little Viggo have ancient names. Children called Sigrid and Viggo were running around in Sweden's Viking days, more than a thousand years ago. Intrepid Viking seafarers ventured far and wide, reaching into Europe, Asia, and beyond. Remnants of Viking culture are treasures in many Swedish museums.

Sigrid uses her bike's headlight a lot in the winter. Located in far-northern Europe, Sweden copes with extremes in daylight and darkness. Some places get only a few hours of sunshine in the winter, and some get none at all!

Lucia Day is one of Sweden's many holidays based on Christian tradition.

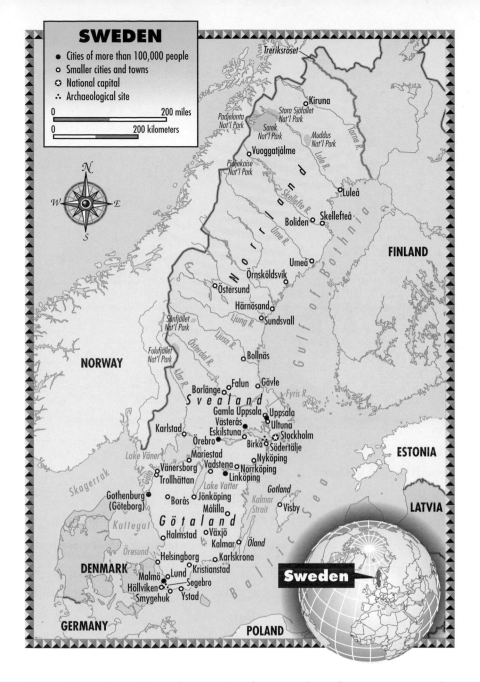

The Church of Sweden, a Lutheran church, was once the national religion. Now people of all religions are free to practice their faith. However, many Swedes today are secular, or nonreligious.

In Sweden, fathers are guaranteed at least two months of time off from their jobs when their children are young. About 85 percent of fathers take parental leave.

Traditional Values

Equality, freedom, openness, and respect for others are core values in Sweden. These values play out in many ways. One example is the freedom that Sigrid's parents have in making child-care decisions. Employers recognize that both parents play important roles in raising a child. Another example is Sweden's openness to immigrants. About one-seventh of the nation's population came from other countries.

Sweden has been called a welfare state because residents enjoy so many benefits. They pay little or nothing for education, health care, and many other basic needs. Taxes are high, but so are people's feelings of satisfaction and security. Sweden's economy is one of the strongest in the world. Its high-tech industries and exports are booming. The nation's military costs are very low, too. Committed to peace, Sweden has not taken part in international wars for two hundred years.

Sweden's political landscape began shifting in the early 2000s. New voices suggest that traditional values must adjust to twenty-first-century challenges. Life in Sweden may be a bit different when Sigrid and Viggo grow up. But they will probably still enjoy their cozy Fridays!

About 85 percent of Swedes live in urban areas.

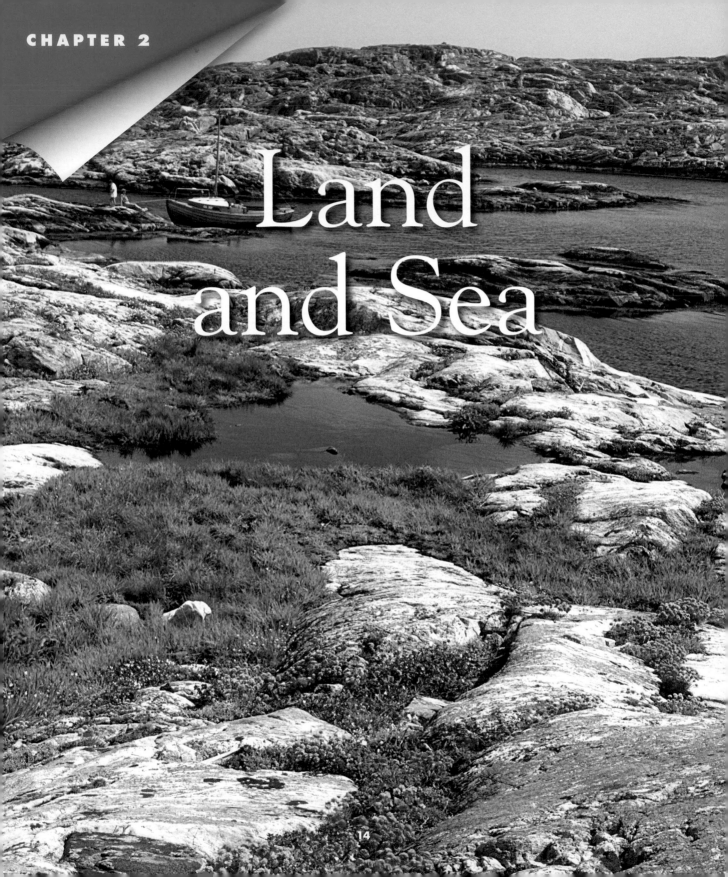

CHAPTER 2

Land and Sea

SWEDEN IS A LAND OF RUGGED FORESTS, BROAD plains, rocky coasts, sparkling lakes, and icy mountains. It is part of a larger region of northern Europe known as Scandinavia. Sweden, Norway, and Denmark are always considered Scandinavian countries. Some experts include Finland and Iceland in Scandinavia, too. Sweden is also considered one of the Nordic countries. The Nordic countries are these same five nations, plus their territories.

Sweden shares the Scandinavian Peninsula with Norway. Sweden is connected by land with only two other countries. Norway borders Sweden to the west, and Finland lies to Sweden's northeast. Sweden is long from north to south and narrow from east to west. In size, it is a bit larger than the U.S. state of California.

Surrounding Waterways

Water surrounds Sweden on the east, south, and southwest. These waters were like highways for Viking ships. Sweden's largest cities grew up along the coast. The east and south

Opposite: **In summer, flowers brighten the rocky west coast of Sweden.**

Ships with cargo packed into giant containers travel from Sweden across the Baltic Sea to other parts of Europe.

coasts face the Baltic Sea and its northern arm, the Gulf of Bothnia. Stockholm, the capital and largest city, lies on the Baltic coast. Sweden has traded with countries in the Baltic region for centuries. It was easy to sail between Sweden and Baltic neighbors such as Russia, Estonia, Latvia, Lithuania, Poland, Germany, and Denmark. Ship traffic among the Baltic nations is still heavy today.

The Baltic Sea curves around southwestern Sweden, where its waters pass through the Danish Straits. These are narrow water channels between Sweden and Denmark. The two countries are so close that people can take a bridge from Malmö, Sweden, to Copenhagen, Denmark.

Southwestern Sweden faces two bodies of water, called the Kattegat and the Skagerrak. They connect with the North Sea, part of the North Atlantic Ocean. Gothenburg, Sweden's largest port and second-largest city, lies along the Kattegat.

Sweden's Geographic Features

Area: 173,860 square miles (450,295 sq km)

Highest Elevation: Mount Kebnekaise, 6,926 feet (2,111 m) above sea level

Lowest Elevation: Lake Hammarsjö, 7.9 feet (2.4 m) below sea level

Greatest Distance North to South: 978 miles (1,574 km)

Greatest Distance East to West: 310 miles (499 km)

Largest Lake: Lake Väner (below), 2,131 square miles (5,519 sq km)

Longest River: Klar, about 200 miles (320 km) in Sweden

Highest Recorded Temperature: 100.4°F (38°C) in Målilla on June 29, 1947, and in Ultuna on July 9, 1933

Lowest Recorded Temperature: −62.7°F (−52.6°C) in Vuoggatjålme on February 2, 1966

Least Daylight in the Winter: Malmö, 7 hours, 2 minutes on December 21; Kiruna, 22 days with no sunrise

Most Daylight in the Summer: Malmö, 17 hours, 31 minutes on June 21; Kiruna, 50 days with no sunset

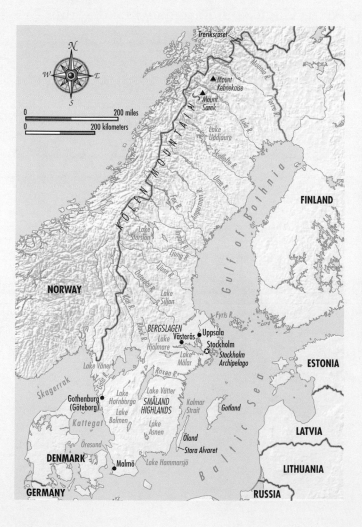

How Far North?

Sweden lies farther north than any point in the United States except for Alaska. Sweden's southernmost point is Smygehuk, a fishing village on the Baltic Sea. Smygehuk is farther north than the central Canadian city of Edmonton, Alberta, and about as northerly as the city of Ketchikan, Alaska.

About 15 percent of Sweden's land area lies north of the Arctic Circle. The Arctic Circle is an imaginary line that runs through the Earth's northern regions. North of the Arctic Circle, in the Arctic region, temperatures are often extremely cold. This is the traditional homeland of Sweden's Sámi

In northern Sweden, snow usually remains on the ground from October until May.

people. Sweden's northernmost point is Treriksröset, the point where the borders of Sweden, Norway, and Denmark meet. The nearest city is Kiruna, Sweden's northernmost town.

Regions, Lands, and Provinces

People often speak in terms of northern Sweden, central Sweden, and southern Sweden. These regions are not evenly divided sections of the country. Northern Sweden usually refers to the northern 50 to 60 percent of the country. Central and southern Sweden are each about half of the remaining land. This informal division is based on Sweden's traditional lands. These three parts of the country are Norrland, Svealand, and Götaland. Norrland, meaning Northlands, covers the northern three-fifths of the country. Because of its chilly climate, Norrland is sparsely populated. Svealand, in central Sweden, means Land of the Svear, an early name for the inhabitants. Svealand was the original, core

Looking at Sweden's Cities

Stockholm, the capital of Sweden, is also its largest city, with a population of 1,372,565 in 2010. Gothenburg (below), or Göteborg in Swedish, is the country's second-largest city, with a population of 549,839. It lies on the west coast, where the Göta River flows into the sea. This location has made Gothenburg the largest port city in Scandinavia.

King Gustav II Adolf founded Gothenburg in 1621, and Dutch immigrants settled the city and designed it with many canals. In the 1700s, wealthy traders built stately stone houses along the canals. Avenyn is the main city street. It passes the Gothenburg Opera House and ends at the Gothenburg Museum of Art. The city is

proud of its blend of modern and historic architecture. The ultramodern Nordstan is Scandinavia's largest shopping mall. In the historic Haga district, cafés and wooden houses line the cobblestone streets. Other attractions are the Gothenburg Botanical Garden and Liseberg amusement park.

Warmed by ocean currents, Gothenburg enjoys a mild climate. High temperatures in the summer average around 68 degrees Fahrenheit (20 degrees Celsius), while average low temperatures in the winter are around 25°F (−4°C). Residents get about 18 hours of daylight in midsummer but only about 6.5 hours at midwinter.

Malmö (above) is the third-largest city in Sweden, with a population of 280,415. Located near the southern tip of Sweden, Malmö was part of Denmark for centuries and became a leading trade center. It was not until 1658 that Malmö became part of Sweden. The city's Kockums shipyard, which opened in 1840, helped make Malmö a booming industrial town. When the shipyard closed in 1986, thousands of workers lost their jobs.

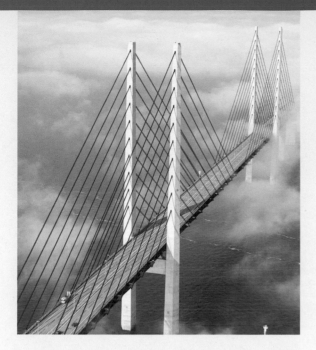

Many innovations helped the city revive. Malmö University opened in 1998. The year 2000 saw the opening of the Öresund Bridge (above), connecting Malmö with Copenhagen, Denmark, across the Öresund Strait. Notable sites are the Modern Museum, the Malmö Opera, the boardwalk along the Western Harbor, and Saint Peter's Church, built in the 1300s. The Turning Torso (see facing page), a skyscraper built in a twisting shape, is the tallest building in Sweden.

Malmö gets about 17.5 daylight hours at midsummer and 7 hours at midwinter. Its climate is mild. High temperatures in the summer average around 70°F (21°C), and winter lows average 27°F (-3°C).

Uppsala, with 140,454 residents, is the nation's fourth-largest city. Located north of Stockholm in east-central Sweden, it is the most northerly of Sweden's large cities. The Fyris River divides the city into its historic western section and its business and residential eastern section.

Uppsala University (right), Scandinavia's oldest university, was founded in 1477. The scientist Carl Linnaeus once taught there. Today the university is a major research center, well known for its medical research. Uppsala Cathedral, built in 1435, is northern Europe's largest cathedral. Uppsala is also the seat of the archbishop of Uppsala, head of the Church of Sweden. Another landmark is Uppsala Castle, home of several Swedish kings and now home to the Uppsala Art Museum. Perched high on a ridge, the castle overlooks much of the city below. Just north of Uppsala is Gamla Uppsala, or Old Uppsala. During the age of the Vikings, its temple was a center of worship for the Nordic religion.

Summertime in Uppsala is mild, and winters are cold. The average high temperature in July is 73°F (23°C). In February, the coldest month, the average low is 21°F (-6°C). Lying farther north than Sweden's other large cities, Uppsala experiences more extremes in daylight hours. Midsummer brings almost 19 hours of daylight, while the sun in midwinter is up for less than 6 hours.

Sarek National Park is a vast stretch of remote wilderness. There are no trails, so visitors must be adventurous to trek through it.

region of Sweden. Later conquests and mergers added the rest of the country. Stockholm and Uppsala are the largest cities in Svealand. Götaland is the southernmost land. It is also the most densely populated. Gothenburg and Malmö, Sweden's second- and third-largest cities, are in Götaland.

Geographic Features

Northern Sweden is a land of forests and snowcapped mountains, with rolling hills, swift-flowing rivers, and many lakes. The huge province of Lappland covers almost half of this region. In the west, forming the border between Sweden and Norway, are the Kölen Mountains. Among these peaks are many glaciers, or mountain-like rivers of ice. In the far north is Mount Kebnekaise, Sweden's highest point, which rises to 6,926 feet (2,111 meters) above sea level. Part of this mountain is a glacier. As the glacier gradually melts, the mountain gets shorter. Mount Sarek, Sweden's second-highest mountain, is surrounded by Sarek National Park. Scattered among the park's many peaks are about one hundred glaciers. Farther east, the land is hilly and densely forested. Many rivers flow toward the southeast, carving out deep valleys and long lakes.

Sweden's land gradually slopes downward from the mountains toward the coast. The lowlands of central Sweden have fertile plains for farming, as well as lush forests. Lake Väner, Sweden's largest lake, is in this region. So are several other large lakes, including lakes Vätter, Mälar, and Hjälmare. Stockholm lies at the point where Lake Mälar flows into the Baltic Sea. The Stockholm Archipelago is a long cluster of islands off the coast of Stockholm, stretching into the Baltic

The Stockholm Archipelago consists of about thirty thousand islands and islets.

Sea. There are about thirty thousand islands in the archipelago. Some are large, populated by fishers and farmers, and others are little rocky outcrops.

South of this region are the Småland Highlands. The soil there is coarse and rocky, making for poor farmland. Forests of pine and spruce grow there, and the hills and rivers are popular vacation areas. Gotland, Sweden's largest island, lies off the coast of Småland. South of Småland is the densely populated province of Skåne. The Skåne plains are Sweden's southernmost region. The soil in Skåne is rich, making it the country's top farming area. Forests once covered this region, but most have been cleared for farming.

Skåne is a patchwork quilt of farmland.

The Midnight Sun

Northern Sweden is sometimes called the Land of the Midnight Sun. In the summer, weeks go by with no sunset. The sun shines around the clock. The opposite effect occurs in the winter, when the sun doesn't appear for days on end. This is called the polar night.

These shifts in light and darkness happen because the earth's axis is tilted. That tilt causes the seasons. As the earth circles the sun over the course of a year, the North Pole tilts toward the sun in the summer and away from the sun in the winter. Because of this, the daylight hours get longer in the summer and shorter in the winter. These differences in daylight become more extreme the closer one gets to the pole.

In Sweden's far-northern town of Kiruna, the sun does not rise for about three weeks in winter. In the summer, the sun stays above the horizon for about seven weeks in a row! Even

The midnight sun sits just above the horizon in Kiruna during the summer. Many people have trouble sleeping during the period of time when the sun is always up.

A woman soaks up the sun in the southern Swedish town of Mariefred. In July, the warmest month in Mariefred, the average high temperature is 73°F (23°C).

in southern Sweden, people experience daylight extremes. For example, June 21, when the sun stays up the longest, is a very long day for people in the southern city of Malmö. They see the sun rise around 4:30 a.m. and set at almost 10:00 p.m. On December 21, Malmö gets its least daylight, barely seven hours. The sun breaks over the horizon around 8:30 a.m. and sets just after 3:30 p.m.

Climate

Even though Sweden lies so far north, much of the country has a mild climate. This is in part caused by the Gulf Stream, a strong ocean current that carries warm water northward from the area near the U.S. state of Florida and across the Atlantic to northern Europe. In southern Sweden, winds blowing off the sea also protect the land from temperature extremes. Southern Sweden enjoys a pleasant summer. In July, the warmest month, Stockholm's average daily high is 72°F (22°C). Winters are mild, too, with an average daily high temperature in January of 31°F (–1°C). Malmö, in the far south, has warmer winters and cooler summers.

In the north, the Kölen Mountains block the warming sea breezes. Winters there can be bitterly cold, with temperatures dropping as low as –40°F (–40°C). Far-northern Kiruna has an average daily high temperature of only 12°F (–11°C) in January. Kiruna's summers can actually be warm. The average high temperature in July is 64°F (18°C).

Every year, Sweden gets about 20 to 31 inches (50 to 80 centimeters) of precipitation. That is moisture in the form of rain, snow, sleet, and hail. August and September are the rainiest months, with the most rain falling in the southwest and the northern mountains. Sweden's snowy season is shorter in the south and longer in the north. In the south, snow falls from about December through March, while in the north, the first snows come in October and the last in May. Although the snow is rough for drivers, it's a welcome sight for skiers and snowmobilers!

In Sweden, people sometimes snowmobile for fun. Other times, it's just a way to get around.

CHAPTER 3

Wild Sweden

SWEDEN'S DIVERSE LANDSCAPE IS TEEMING WITH wildlife. The country's grassy plains, shadowy forests, bleak mountainsides, and rocky coasts make ideal habitats for a variety of creatures.

Trees and Flowers

Conifers, or cone-bearing trees, cover more than half of Sweden. Most of these trees are spruce and pine. Conifers keep their leaves year-round, while deciduous trees shed their leaves in the fall. Southern Sweden has many deciduous trees, such as beech, oak, elm, ash, and maple. The thickest forests grow in the north, where birch, aspen, and ash mix with the conifers.

High in the mountains is a point called the tree line. It occurs at about 1,600 feet (500 meters). No trees grow above that elevation because the climate is too cold. Only low shrubs, lichens, and mosses are found beyond the tree line. They come to life in the summer when the surface soil thaws. Many flowering plants light up the high meadows with color.

Linnaeus's Twinflower

Sweden has no official national flower. Unofficially, however, many people consider the twinflower to be the national flower. Its delicate, pink, bell-shaped flowers grow in pairs and smell a little like vanilla. With the scientific name *Linnaea borealis*, the twinflower was named after Swedish botanist Carl Linnaeus. He found abundant twinflowers while exploring northern Sweden, and they became his favorite plant. After the Swedish king made Linnaeus a member of the nobility, Linnaeus featured the twinflower on his coat of arms. Each of Sweden's provinces has a provincial flower, just as most U.S. states have a state flower, and the twinflower is the provincial flower of Småland, where Linnaeus was born.

Fields in the south are ablaze with wildflowers, too. There are snowdrops, wild pansies, blue comfrey, yellow chamomile, meadow buttercups, and Iceland poppies, to name just a few. After a bleak winter, they are a welcome sight! The southern province of Skåne and the island of Öland off southeastern Sweden are known for their orchid meadows. Visitors from around the world come to see the orchids in bloom. Orchid lovers enjoy Gothenburg's international orchid show, held every two years.

In the spring and summer, people enjoy exploring the forests for edible plants. They find lingonberries, blueberries, raspberries, and cloudberries. They might pick wild mushrooms or gather acorns from oak trees and beechnuts from beech trees. Some people hunt for a prickly plant called the nettle, or stinging nettle. They use the leaves and stems to make Sweden's traditional nettle soup.

Birds of the Forests and Marshes

In the spring, many bird species pass through Sweden on their yearly migrations. They are flying north from their winter homes in Africa, Asia, and southern Europe. Thousands of cranes descend upon Lake Hornborga in southwestern Sweden in the spring. They do a kind of dance, fanning their wings out and springing into the air. After a month, they continue on to their nesting grounds in northern Sweden. The lake's marshy environment also shelters grebes, whooper swans, ospreys, and sea eagles.

The courtship dance of the black grouse is another spectacular sight. This grouse is native to the central forests. Sweden's wood grouse is the world's largest grouse species. It, too, puts on a courtship dance—strutting, gurgling, and fanning its tail. Both forest and wetland birds inhabit the Black River valley area of central Sweden. Besides grouse, this region is home to three-toed, gray-headed, and black woodpeckers drumming on the tree trunks. As evening falls, out come the pygmy owls, Ural owls, and great gray owls. Other birds of prey found in the region include hen harriers, great gray shrikes, and golden eagles.

One of Sweden's largest birds of prey, the golden eagle, has a wingspan of more than 6 feet (2 m). It is known in Swedish as the *kungsörn*, or king's eagle. It usually feeds on rodents and other small animals, but golden eagles have taken prey as large as foxes and young deer.

The pygmy owl grows only about 7 inches (18 cm) high. It hunts prey such as mice, lemmings, and small birds.

Mammals Large and Small

Brown bears roam the forests and mountains of northern Sweden. They are the country's largest predators. In the autumn, they gobble up berries to store energy for their winter hibernation. Brown bears are shy and avoid humans. However, they might attack if they sense a threat to themselves or their cubs.

Sometimes at night, people hear wolves letting loose with spine-chilling howls. These predators travel in packs of ten to fifteen. They hunt animals as big as reindeer, as well as smaller animals such as dogs, sheep, and calves. By the 1970s, hunters had killed so many wolves that they were almost extinct in Sweden. Then wolf hunting was banned. Within a few years, more wolves crossed over from Finland and Russia. By 2013, there were about 270 wolves in Sweden. Because wolves were killing so many animals, the government has allowed some hunting again. However, conservationists strongly oppose wolf hunting.

The lynx is Sweden's only wildcat. Lynx live in northern and central Sweden, though people rarely see these shy

Lynx have extraordinary hearing and eyesight. They can spot a mouse from 250 feet (75 m) away.

predators. Wolverines are another predator. They are related to badgers, but they are much larger and have a bushy tail. Sweden's wolverines prey on reindeer in the winter and smaller mammals in the summer. They are scavengers, feeding on dead animals they find. Most wolverines live in northern Sweden, but they are gradually spreading southward.

Sweden's largest mammals are moose. The males grow huge antlers in the spring and shed them in the winter. Moose are fast runners and good swimmers. They often wander across roadways, so warning signs are posted by the roadsides in wilderness areas. Bergslagen Forest in central Sweden is a great place to see large moose herds.

Reindeer herds range across northern Sweden. Both male and female reindeer grow new antlers every year. Skin with tiny hairs covers the antlers while they are growing. This

Sweden's Moose

Sweden has no official animal symbol. However, the moose is generally considered the national animal. Moose are the largest members of the deer family. During mating season, two males may fight over a female, bashing each other with their antlers. People in Sweden have hunted moose for thousands of years. Antlers found in a hut at the Stora Alvaret site on the island of Öland date from about 6000 BCE. Moose hunting is common in Sweden today, too, and moose meat is a popular food in the north.

makes the antlers look fuzzy. Herding reindeer is a traditional way of life for Sweden's Sámi people. Reindeer fur, meat, bones, and antlers are all put to good use.

Reindeer eat grass, moss, ferns, lichen, and whatever else grows in the frigid north.

Reindeer and the Sámi

Reindeer are a deep-seated part of the culture of Sweden's Sámi people. Today, more than fifty Sámi communities in Sweden are engaged in reindeer herding, as their ancestors were for hundreds of years. As the seasons change, the Sámi move their herds to new grazing lands. Herding involves many activities, such as caring for new calves and protecting the herd from wolves and other predators. The reindeer provide milk, meat, hides, and other products—not only for home use but also as profitable trade goods. For many Sámi families, reindeer herding is their major source of income. Over the years, the Sámi have faced many legal challenges over grazing rights. As more land is cleared and developed, the Sámi have been pushed off their traditional grazing lands. The Sámi continue to fight to protect their way of life.

Roe deer, beavers, wild boars, hares, and voles are some of Sweden's smaller mammals. Roe deer and moose sometimes wander near people's homes.

Water Creatures

Cod, mackerel, salmon, pike, and herring are plentiful off Sweden's coasts. Whales and porpoises can be seen leaping in graceful arches in the waters off the west coast. Some have even been spotted toward the east, in the Baltic Sea. However, Sweden's most visible water creatures are seals.

Gray seals inhabit the Baltic coastal areas, especially along the Stockholm Archipelago. They are Sweden's largest seals, growing up to 10 feet (3 m) long. Hundreds of seals gather along the shore in seal rookeries, places where they breed and raise pups. In February, a female gives birth to one pup, often while floating on an ice floe. Hunting seals in the Baltic region is banned by an international agreement called the Helsinki Convention. Once in decline, populations of these awesome creatures are on the rise again.

Gray seals relax on a rock in the Stockholm Archipelago.

CHAPTER 4

Vikings, Kings, and the Modern World

THOUSANDS OF YEARS AGO, VAST STRETCHES OF HARD-packed snow and ice covered much of Europe, including all of what is now Sweden. A warm period around 12,000 BCE began melting the ice in southern Sweden. Then deer, moose, and other animals began to arrive, followed by nomadic hunters. A village at Segebro, near Malmö, is Sweden's earliest known settlement. Scientists believe people lived there around 9000 BCE.

As the ice melted and exposed more land, more people moved to the area. Some were hunters, while others made a living by fishing. They grouped together into tribes. By around 2500 BCE, some Swedish tribes were farming and raising cattle. Soon Swedes developed a thriving trade with people on the European mainland, exchanging furs and other goods for bronze. By 50 BCE, Swedes were trading with the Roman Empire. The Roman historian Tacitus described a powerful Scandinavian people called the Suiones or Svear. The land of the Svear was Sverige, the Swedish name for Sweden today.

Opposite: **A stone from the 800s shows Viking ships at sea and warriors fighting.**

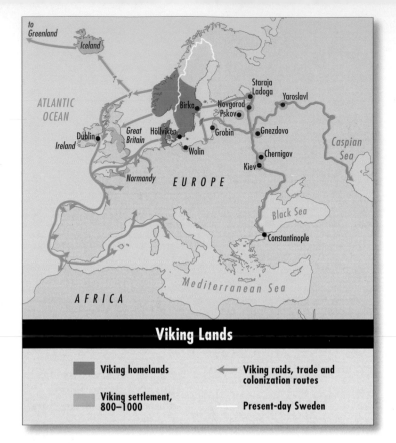

to Greenland
Iceland
ATLANTIC OCEAN
Staraja Ladoga
Yaroslavl
Birka
Novgorod
Pskov
Great Britain
Dublin
Ireland
Höllviken
Grobin
Gnezdovo
Wolin
Chernigov
Kiev
Caspian Sea
Normandy
EUROPE
Black Sea
Constantinople
Mediterranean Sea
AFRICA

Viking Lands

Viking homelands

Viking settlement, 800–1000

Viking raids, trade and colonization routes

Present-day Sweden

Vikings and Early Christians

Sweden's Viking age began around 800 CE. The Vikings, or Norsemen, were seagoing people. In their swift, wooden longships, they raided lands thousands of miles from home. Viking leaders were chieftains from Sweden, Norway, and Denmark. At home, the Vikings were farmers. Perhaps because of overpopulation, they took to the sea, trading with and sometimes plundering towns along the coasts. Each Viking group had its own preferred territory. Norwegians sailed north and west to lands such as Greenland and Ireland. Danes went to England and France.

Swedish Vikings turned toward the east. They set up the town of Birka, on the Baltic seacoast. Founded in the 700s, it is considered Sweden's first town. Birka was a good launching point for voyages. From Birka, the Vikings took over the Baltic Sea region and then moved deep into Russia and neighboring lands. There they carved out trade routes and established settlements. Vikings even led raids into western Europe.

A Viking group called the Rus pushed into land as far as the Byzantine Empire, with its capital at Constantinople (present-day Istanbul, Turkey). According to an Arab traveler of the 900s, the Rus were "tall as date palms, blonde and

Many museums in Sweden feature exhibits about Viking life. Stockholm's National Historical Museum has the world's largest Viking exhibition, with more than four thousand artifacts, including tools, toys, harness mounts (left), and weapons.

Fotevikens Museum is an archaeological open-air museum that recreates daily life in a Viking community. It is located in Höllviken in southwest Sweden, once the site of a Viking trading post. As visitors stroll through the town, they can explore houses built as they were in Viking times. Costumed villagers go about their daily lives, practicing traditional Viking crafts.

The Viking town of Birka was founded in the late 700s on the island of Björkö in Stockholm's Lake Mälar. Archaeologists are still digging up remains of the old settlement, which was once home to as many as one thousand Vikings and foreign traders.

ruddy," the men wearing "a garment, which covers one side of the body." Rus leaders ruled Russia for about two hundred years, until the late 1000s.

During the Viking period, Swedish people followed Norse religions, which had many gods. A Christian monk named Ansgar arrived in 829, hoping to spread Christianity. He opened a church in Birka but did not have much success converting people to his religion. For almost two hundred years, the old and new religions struggled against each other. Finally, around 1000, King Olof Skötkonung accepted Christianity. Sweden eventually became a Christian land. The Viking era ended as Christianity took hold.

Rune Stones

Rune stones are large rocks that are inscribed and are usually found standing upright. The inscriptions are written in runes, or letters used before the Latin alphabet was adopted. The rune stone tradition began in the 300s CE and lasted until the 1100s. Vikings erected rune stones throughout Scandinavia and in many of the places they visited. Typically, a rune stone commemorates an important event or honors the memory of a dead person. Others tell of intrepid Viking voyages. Sweden may have as many as 2,500 rune stones, far more than any other country has. The spectacular Lingsberg rune stones, north of Stockholm, are covered with text and animal drawings.

Unified Sweden

Uniting Sweden into one kingdom was a long process. Each province's king claimed to be the ruler of all of Sweden. Some historians say King Olof was the first king to rule over Sweden's main provinces of Svealand and Götaland. Others say King Sverker first united these provinces in the 1100s. Sweden added much of what is now Finland to its kingdom in the 1200s.

Meanwhile, Swedish merchants carried on a thriving international trade. Their exports included furs, iron ore, and forest products. Soon Sweden was mostly trading with the Hanseatic League. This was a powerful trading partnership centered in Lübeck, in northern Germany. Over time, the Hanseatic League dominated trade in the Baltic region, which had once been controlled by Sweden. German traders began to set up operations in Swedish towns. Trading towns flourished, though many Swedes resented the German traders' power.

At the same time, civil wars racked the Swedish kingdom. Rival families often fought to take the throne. Various nobles aligned themselves with Norway or Denmark to fight against the king. The king also made alliances to fight the nobles. In 1388, Swedish nobles called on Queen Margaret of Denmark and Norway for help. The queen's armies fought their way to peace. In 1397, Sweden, Norway, and Denmark formed the Kalmar Union under Queen Margaret's rule. The three kingdoms signed the Treaty of Kalmar in Sweden's Kalmar Castle.

Kalmar Union

—— Present-day border

Malmö had more than five thousand residents in the 1400s, making it the second-largest city in the Kalmar Union. This image shows the city in the following century.

Kalmar Castle

Magnificent Kalmar Castle began as one round, fortified tower in the 1100s. Situated in the southeastern town of Kalmar, it overlooked the Kalmar Strait (Kalmarsund) facing Denmark. A century later, King Magnus Ladulås built a wall and more towers around the original tower. The castle's greatest event was the signing of the Kalmar Union in 1397. In the 1500s, Gustav Vasa and his sons converted the castle into a lavishly decorated palace in the Renaissance style. After the Kalmar War and a fire in the 1600s, the castle fell into ruin. Later restorations returned it to its former beauty.

Independent Sweden

According to the treaty, the Kalmar Union was to last forever, but this was not to be. In Sweden, conflicts raged between those people who favored the Kalmar Union and those who wanted Swedish independence. The breaking point came in 1520, when the Danish king Christian II executed eighty Swedish nobles who opposed the Kalmar Union. This became known as the Stockholm Bloodbath. One angry nobleman, Gustav Vasa, then led Sweden's war of liberation (1521–1523). Vasa's victories ended the Kalmar Union and established Sweden as a kingdom in its own right.

Vasa was crowned King Gustav I, the first king of independent Sweden. Gustav made many changes. He broke the power of the Hanseatic League, giving Swedish merchants the trade privileges they had lost. He also established the Church of Sweden as the national church under his authority. At this time, the Protestant Reformation was sweeping through Europe.

Gustav Vasa (1496?–1560) is honored as the father of modern Sweden. After his father was executed in the Stockholm Bloodbath, Vasa led Sweden's war of liberation (1521–1523) against Denmark and Norway. He reigned as King Gustav I of Sweden from 1523 until his death. As king, Gustav introduced hereditary monarchy, which is still in effect today. Sweden's National Day, June 6, marks the day in 1523 when Gustav was elected king.

Martin Luther of Germany had started the movement in 1517. Luther and other reformers objected to some practices in the Roman Catholic Church. They challenged the church's authority and many church teachings. This led to the founding of the

This painting by Swedish artist Julius Kronberg shows King Gustav I receiving the first Swedish translation of the Bible.

Lutheran Church and other Protestant churches. In 1593, the Church of Sweden became a Lutheran church.

Sweden grew to be a great European power in the 1600s. King Gustav II Adolf began his reign in 1611 and waged many wars. Under his leadership, Sweden came to control much of the Baltic region, including parts of Russia and Poland. Sweden became one of the largest nations in Europe. This period of Swedish power is known as the Swedish Empire. King Charles XII carried the wars on into the 1700s. Finally Denmark, Russia, Poland, and other allies joined forces against Sweden. They waged the Great Northern War (1700–1721), killing Charles in 1718 and bringing the Swedish Empire to an end. Sweden was forced to give up huge territories it had once ruled.

The Age of Freedom

After King Charles XII's death, Sweden began to change its governing structure. An assembly called the Riksdag of the Estates had been established in the 1400s. Its power was second only to the king's. But Charles had ruled as an absolute monarch, sharing power with no one. In 1718, the Riksdag met and decided to make Sweden a constitutional monarchy. Under the Riksdag's new constitution,

Swedish Empire

- Sweden in 1560
- Areas gained by 1582
- Areas gained by 1628
- Areas gained by 1645
- Areas gained by 1660
- Present-day border

Lapland

Trondheim
Jämtland
Karelia
Finland
Ingria
Sweden
Dagö
Estonia
Bohuslän
Ösel
Halland
Livonia
Gotland
Skåne
Bornholm
Memel
Bremen
Pillau
West
Elbing
Pomerania
Wismar

the king had much less power, and the Riksdag governed the country. This introduced a period called the Age of Freedom.

The Age of Freedom was a time of great political chaos and confusion. At the same time, industry and trade flourished. Swedish trading ships sailed as far as China and India. At home, shipbuilding, textile production, and ironworking industries blossomed. Sweden became one of the world's largest exporters of iron. Ordinary people's lives improved as social classes became less important. Peasants gained the right to buy land instead of having to work on wealthy people's estates. Farm products sold at good prices, so farmers prospered. Common people were also able to hold government positions once held only by nobles. The Age of Freedom ended in 1772, when King Gustav III assumed absolute power.

Workers at a Swedish iron foundry in the 1700s. The wheels were used to flatten the metal into sheets.

Sweden fought along with Russia, Austria, and Prussia against Napoleon's French troops at the Battle of Leipzig in what is now Germany. More than five hundred thousand troops took part in the battle.

War and Decline

Like many other European countries, Sweden feared the power of French emperor Napoleon Bonaparte. In 1805, King Gustav IV Adolf joined forces with other countries to fight France. For Sweden, the wars had devastating results. Sweden was forced to give up Finland to Russia in 1809. Many government officials in Sweden considered Gustav IV Adolf a poor leader. The loss of Finland was the last straw. A group of officials and army officers overthrew Gustav, and he was forced to leave the throne. A new constitution, the Instrument of Government of 1809, again reduced the king's authority and increased the Riksdag's powers. Another outcome of the war was that Denmark gave up Norway to Sweden in 1814. This union of Sweden and Norway under the Swedish king would last until 1905.

The Napoleonic Wars had brought Sweden's economy to a standstill. The wars had interrupted overseas trade, so merchants were unable to do as much business as they had before. In addition, most Swedes lived by farming, and the growing population meant there was less farmland to go around. Beginning in the mid-1800s, countless shiploads of Swedish families emigrated, or left the country. By 1930, about 1.5 million Swedes had moved away. Most went to the United States in hopes of starting a new life.

Emigrants make their way to the port at Gothenburg. From there, they sailed to the United States.

Recovery and Social Reform

Back in Sweden, social and cultural movements were seizing people's minds and hearts. One was the free-church movement, a reaction against the national Church of Sweden. Another interest was the temperance movement, aimed at curbing the consumption of alcohol. Yet another issue was equal rights for women. Gradually, women were given greater and greater rights. For example, in 1845, women gained the same rights that men had regarding inheritance, and women were allowed to vote in local elections in 1862.

In the late nineteenth and early twentieth centuries, many Swedes were trying to create a more equitable society. In 1902, a large strike was held in Sweden, with protesters demanding that more people be allowed to vote.

Industry began to grow again in the late 1800s. New machinery was introduced, as well as new methods of producing iron and steel. The development of labor unions and the founding of the Social Democratic Party went hand in hand with industrial growth. These groups worked closely together through the twentieth century and beyond. New laws in the early 1900s provided for old-age benefits and insurance against workplace injuries.

In the 1930s, Sweden began considering the idea of *folkhemmet*, meaning "the people's home." This was a view of Swedish society as a true home for its people—a place where everyone's needs were taken care of, whether they were sick, unemployed, elderly, or in need of an education. In such a plan, everyone would contribute, just as if the whole society were a family.

Workers put together Thulin K aircraft at a factory in Landskrona, Sweden, in 1917. The Thulin K was the first plane produced in Sweden.

Vikings, Kings, and the Modern World **51**

Raoul Wallenberg: Wartime Hero

During World War II, it was German policy to round up and kill Jewish people and others who were considered "undesirable," such as Romanis (Gypsies) and the disabled. Raoul Wallenberg was a Swedish businessman and diplomat who helped Jews in Hungary, an ally of Germany, escape this fate.

In order to save Hungarian Jews from being sent to concentration camps, Wallenberg issued them passports that identified them as Swedish citizens. He also rented dozens of buildings in Budapest, Hungary, and flew Swedish flags above them. This made them appear to be official buildings of Sweden, a neutral country, so German forces could not enter them and Hungarian Jews could remain safe inside. He even showed up at trains that were taking Jews to concentration camps, and offered the Jews food and clothing and tried to get them Swedish passports. Through such heroic efforts, Wallenberg helped rescue tens of thousands of Hungarian Jews.

By 1945, forces from the Soviet Union, one of the Allies fighting Germany, had invaded Hungary. Soviet officials arrested Wallenberg, although the circumstances are not clear. According to most reports, he died in a Soviet prison two years later, but his courageous actions were not forgotten.

Foreign Policy

Sweden had not been involved in international wars since 1814. Neighboring countries fought in both World War I (1914–1918) and World War II (1939–1945). Sweden, however, remained neutral. World War II had begun in Europe when Germany invaded Poland, and Germany proceeded to invade other neighboring nations. Sweden's neutrality allowed people threatened by Germany to take refuge in the country. At the same time, however, the Swedes allowed German trains filled with iron ore to cross their territory.

In 1946, when Sweden joined the United Nations (UN), an international organization intended to resolve conflicts, it kept its foreign policy of neutrality. This stance has made Swedish diplomats appealing on the international scene. For example, Sweden's Dag Hammarskjöld was elected UN secretary-general in 1953.

To the Present

Sweden thrived in the years after the end of World War II. Unlike much of Europe, Sweden's infrastructure had not been destroyed during the war. This allowed the country to enjoy rapid economic development. In these years, the Social

Working for Peace

Dag Hammarskjöld (1905–1961) was secretary-general of the United Nations from 1953 until his death in 1961. Born in Jönköping, Hammarskjöld was the youngest son of a former prime minister of Sweden. Even before he finished his university studies, Hammarskjöld began his long career in Swedish government positions.

At the UN, Hammarskjöld worked hard to resolve international tensions such as the Arab–Israeli conflicts. He also supported independence for African states that were colonies of European powers. In 1961, he was on his way to negotiate a cease-fire in the Democratic Republic of the Congo. On the way, his airplane crashed, and he was killed. Many people believed the crash was an assassination, but investigations found no proof of this. Hammarskjöld was awarded the Nobel Peace Prize after his death.

Democrats were in power, and the country's commitment to the welfare of its citizens and public institutions continued to grow. Higher education, health insurance, and pensions for the elderly were expanded.

In the 1950s, many European countries began seeking closer economic cooperation. The European Economic Community was established in 1957. Sweden, however, remained committed to its policy of neutrality and chose not to join. Over the years, as many European countries became ever more closely joined economically and politically, Sweden

Sweden's economy grew quickly after World War II. Here, workers manufacture Volvo cars.

Vad hä om Sv ham utanfö

Ska vi a sämre lkor än ndra?

Ja till eur

Samarbeta eller stå utanför?

Ja till euron!
www.jatilleuron.se

Vad händer om Sverige hamnar utanför?

Ja till euron!
www.jatilleuron.se

feared that it might be left behind. The European Economic Community eventually evolved into the European Union (EU), and Sweden joined in 1995. The EU member countries form a single economic market. Goods can be sent from one country to another without being taxed, and citizens can move freely between the countries and live in whichever country they choose.

Swedish diplomats have taken a leadership role in the EU. Sweden has held the presidency of the Council of the European Union twice, in 2001 and 2009.

Still, Sweden insists on keeping its unique traditions. More than half of EU member nations have adopted the euro as their currency. However, in 2003, Swedish voters rejected the euro in favor of their time-honored krona. Twenty-first century Sweden promises a fascinating face-off between traditions and innovations.

In 2003, Sweden held a referendum on whether to adopt the euro as the nation's currency. The signs shown here ask what will happen if Sweden doesn't join the euro nations.

CHAPTER 5

Ruling the Nation

SWEDEN'S OFFICIAL NAME IS THE KINGDOM OF SWEDEN. This land has had a king for more than two thousand years. Swedish kings were once elected by the people. However, since 1554, the monarchy (kingship) has been hereditary. Today's King Carl XVI Gustaf became king in 1973, following the death of his grandfather.

In the past, only male heirs could ascend to the throne. In 1980, Sweden became the first European country to pass a law requiring the monarchy to pass to the oldest child, regardless of gender. The oldest child of King Carl Gustaf and his wife, Queen Silvia, is Crown Princess Victoria. She is next in line to become Queen of Sweden if her father resigns or when he dies.

Monarch sounds like a powerful position. In Sweden, however, the monarch has no political power. Over the centuries, the king's authority was reduced little by little. By 1974, the monarchy had become a ceremonial position. Now the monarch is officially the head of state, representing Sweden in

Opposite: **King Carl XVI Gustaf reviews an honor guard. All of the king's duties are ceremonial.**

The Swedish Parliament meets in the Parliament House in Gamla Stan, the old town of Stockholm.

formal ceremonies around the world. Instead of a powerful king, Sweden has a constitution, or basic set of laws. Thus, its form of government is called a constitutional monarchy.

The Constitution

"All public power in Sweden proceeds from the people." That's how the first law in Sweden's constitution begins. The constitution puts forth four basic principles, called the Fundamental Laws of the Realm. The first principle is the Instrument of Government, updated in 1974. It sets forth the duties of government officials. Next is the Act of Succession, adopted in 1810. It lays out rules for the royal family and the monarch. The Freedom of the Press Act (1949) guarantees an open society. That is, the people have the right to see any official government documents. Also, people are free to

Princess Victoria, the daughter of King Carl XVI Gustaf, is next in line for the throne. She is shown here with her husband, Prince Daniel.

publish any information they want to publish. A similar law is the Fundamental Law on Freedom of Expression (1992). It extends the free press guarantees to radio and TV broadcasts. Another basic law, the 1974 Riksdag Act, sets forth the work procedures for the Riksdag, or parliament.

The National Flag

The Swedish flag features a yellow cross on a blue background. The cross's vertical bar is slightly left of the center. The cross represents Christianity. It is called the Scandinavian Cross because it appears on the flags of all the Scandinavian countries. The yellow and blue colors come from the Swedish coat of arms of the 1400s, which has three yellow crowns on a blue background. The yellow cross became standard in 1569, when King John III declared that all of Sweden's battle flags should carry a yellow cross. When Sweden and Norway were united (1814–1905), Sweden's flag carried a symbol of the union in the upper left-hand corner. The emblem was removed in 1906 when Sweden officially adopted its national flag.

The National Anthem

"Du Gamla, Du Fria" ("Thou Ancient, Thou Free") is Sweden's national anthem. Richard Dybeck wrote the lyrics in 1844. For the melody, he chose a folk tune from Västmanland province. The anthem mentions the North, rather than Sweden, because an all-Scandinavian movement was strong at the time. Sweden's legislature has never officially adopted this anthem. However, it is widely embraced as the national anthem.

Swedish lyrics

Du gamla, Du fria, Du fjällhöga nord
Du tysta, Du glädjerika sköna!
Jag hälsar Dig, vänaste land uppå jord,
Din sol, Din himmel, Dina ängder gröna.
Din sol, Din himmel, Dina ängder gröna.

Du tronar på minnen från fornstora dar,
då ärat Ditt namn flög över jorden.
Jag vet att Du är och Du blir vad du var.
Ja, jag vill leva jag vill dö i Norden.
Ja, jag vill leva jag vill dö i Norden.

English translation

Thou ancient, thou free and mountainous North
Thou quiet, thou joyful beauty!
I greet thee, most beautiful land upon earth,
Thy sun, Thy sky and meadows green.
Thy sun, Thy sky and meadows green.

Thou rest upon memories of great olden days,
When honored thy name flew across the world,
I know that thou art and will be as thou were,
Yes, I want to live I want to die in the North.
Yes, I want to live I want to die in the North.

The Riksdag

Sweden's national legislature is the Riksdag. It is the country's lawmaking body, similar to the U.S. Congress and the Canadian Parliament. Those two legislatures are bicameral, or made up of two houses. However, the Riksdag is unicameral, with just one house. The 349 Riksdag members are elected to four-year terms. Citizens vote for them in districts divided according to population. Riksdag members vote to choose the Speaker of the Riksdag, who presides over the assembly. They also elect members of various committees.

Members of the Swedish Parliament listen to a translation through headphones as the president of Turkey speaks.

As a member of the EU, Sweden must obey the laws of the EU in addition to its own national laws. Some issues that the Riksdag used to handle are now decided by the EU. Sweden has a voice in the EU's legislative process. It has a representative in the Council of the European Union, part of the EU's lawmaking body.

Leading the Government

Executive power in Sweden rests with the prime minister and a cabinet of about twenty-two ministers. The prime minister

National Government of Sweden

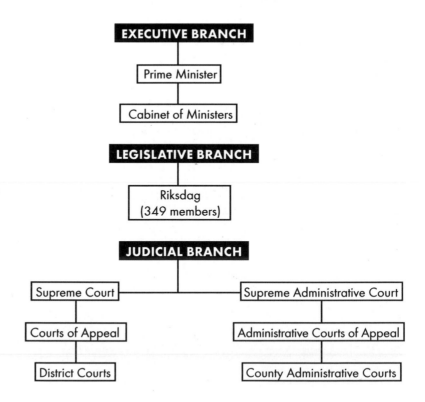

EXECUTIVE BRANCH

Prime Minister

Cabinet of Ministers

LEGISLATIVE BRANCH

Riksdag
(349 members)

JUDICIAL BRANCH

Supreme Court — Supreme Administrative Court

Courts of Appeal — Administrative Courts of Appeal

District Courts — County Administrative Courts

is the head of the government. The Speaker of the Riksdag appoints the prime minister, with the approval of the Riksdag. Usually the prime minister is the leader of the political party that has the majority of members in the Riksdag. The prime minister then appoints the cabinet ministers. Each cabinet minister oversees an important area such as trade, defense, culture, employment, and the environment.

Stefan Löfven (left) became the head of the Social Democratic Party in 2012. The Social Democrats have ruled Sweden the majority of the time since World War II. They are more liberal than the parties currently in power.

Political Parties

Unlike the United States, which has just two political parties, Sweden has many parties. The nation has about eight major parties and more than a dozen minor parties. With so many voices, it is hard for any one party to win a majority in the Riksdag. To solve this problem, several parties often agree to put aside their differences and work together. They form a coalition, and then that coalition forms the next government.

Fredrik Reinfeldt

Fredrik Reinfeldt (1965–) became Sweden's twenty-sixth prime minister in 2006. As chairman of Sweden's Moderate Party, he formed a coalition with three other parties in the Riksdag and declared victory. Before this, the Social Democratic Party had held power for ten years. The Moderate Party has traditionally favored more individual freedoms and less government involvement in business. But Reinfeldt has adopted a practical, collaborative approach and has moved his party more toward the center. In 2010, Reinfeldt won a second four-year term.

Sweden's main political parties fall into two broad categories: left and right. Parties on the left generally favor strong labor unions and equal rights. Parties on the right favor businesses, individual freedoms, and lower taxes. Since extreme views have little support, both sides tend to move toward the middle. As a result, Sweden's largest parties are those that hold center-right or center-left views.

Sweden's center-left Social Democratic Party held power for most of the twentieth century. By 2004, several center-right parties had grown tired of being in the minority. They formed a center-right coalition called the Alliance. This was a partnership of the Moderate Party, the Liberal People's Party, the Center Party, and the Christian Democratic Party. The Alliance won the 2006 election.

Hoping to win back the government, the Social Democrats formed a coalition, too. In 2008, they joined with the Green Party and the Left Party to form the Red-Green coalition.

But the Alliance prevailed again. After adding another party, the Alliance went on to win the 2010 election. Now Swedish citizens and observers worldwide are wondering if the Social Democrats have lost their longstanding grip on Sweden's political scene.

Swedes stand behind curtains to vote. Sweden has one of the world's highest voter turnout rates. About 85 percent of the people eligible to vote usually do so.

Women Rule!

After the 2010 election, about 45 percent of the Riksdag members were women. That's one of the highest female representations in the world. Only Rwanda, Andorra, and Cuba have a higher proportion of women in their national legislatures. In contrast, the Canadian Parliament ranks forty-sixth in the world in female representation in the legislature, and the U.S. Congress ranks seventy-eighth.

The Judicial System

Sweden has two types of courts: the general courts and the administrative courts. The general courts handle criminal and civil cases. General courts are organized on three levels. From bottom to top they are district courts, courts of appeal, and the Supreme Court. Anyone who does not agree with a lower court's decision may appeal it at a higher level. The Supreme Court is the highest court, and its decisions are final.

At least fourteen judges make up the Supreme Court. They do not accept any case that comes before them. Instead, they decide whether to hear a case. This usually depends on whether their decision will set a precedent. That is, they prefer cases involving a legal question that has never been settled clearly before. Five of the judges eventually preside over a case.

The Supreme Court meets in Bonde Palace in Stockholm. The palace was built as a private residence in the 1660s, became a courthouse in 1697, and has housed the Supreme Court since 1949.

Stockholm: The Capital City

Stockholm is considered one of the most beautiful capital cities in the world. It is built on fourteen islands connected by fifty-seven bridges. Walking around the city, people feel close to nature because of the green spaces, sparkling water, and clean air.

Stockholm lies on the southeast coast, at the point where Lake Mälar flows into the Baltic Sea. The city was founded around 1250 and became an important Baltic Sea trading port during the days of the Hanseatic League. Today, Stockholm's metropolitan area is home to more than two million people and is the cultural, economic, and political center of the nation.

The city's architecture reflects both its early history and its modern outlook. The original city center is Gamla Stan (Old Town), situated mainly on the island of Stadsholmen. Many of this sector's well-preserved buildings are hundreds of years old. Cobbled streets and narrow alleyways also remain from the early days. Here stand the Royal Palace, the Riksdag building, the Church of Saint Nicholas, and the German Church.

Norrmalm, the city's main business, financial, and shopping district, lies north of Gamla Stan. Its large public plaza, Sergels Torg, is considered the center of Stockholm. The Royal Swedish Opera House is one of Norrmalm's notable buildings. On a peninsula in western Norrmalm stands Sweden's National Museum of Fine Arts. City Hall, in the district of Kungsholmen, is where the annual Nobel Prize banquet is held.

South of Gamla Stan is the Södermalm district. Workers' cottages once clung to its cliffs and rocky hills. Today, Södermalm is a trendy district of clothing boutiques, art galleries, and vintage goods. Its tallest building is Söder Torn, an ultramodern, high-rise apartment building.

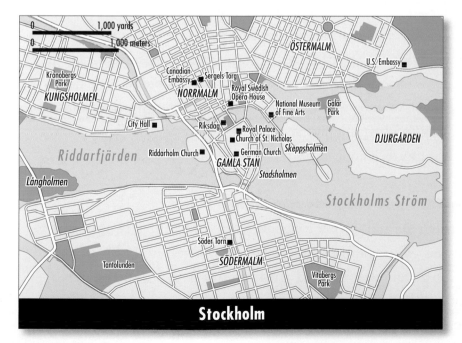

Stockholm

The 101 members of the Stockholm City Council meet in this room in the Stockholm City Hall.

The administrative courts deal with cases that have to do with public administration. These might concern citizenship issues, minorities' rights, local government measures, church and state issues, and so on. Administrative courts, too, have three levels: county administrative courts, administrative courts of appeal, and the Supreme Administrative Court. This court also has fourteen judges, and five of them hear a case.

Regional and Local Government

At the regional level, Sweden is divided into twenty-one counties. The county system was established in 1634. Before that, Sweden was divided into twenty-five provinces. Each province had its own laws, character, culture, and in some cases, religious beliefs. Many of today's counties have the same names and borders as the provinces had. The concept of the provinces has never completely died out. Many Swedish people still speak in terms of provinces.

Today, each county has a governor appointed by the national government, and a county council whose members are elected. Council members oversee matters that are too extensive for local governments to handle on their own, such as health care and regional roadways. County councils also have the right to charge income taxes.

Two hundred ninety municipalities govern on the local level. Municipal governments have a wide range of responsibilities. They deal with local issues such as city planning, housing, schools, streets, sewage, water supply, public assistance, child welfare, and elder care. Like the counties, municipalities can collect income taxes. Citizens elect the members of their municipal assemblies. Both regional and local elections are held at the same time as the parliamentary elections.

Caring for rural roads is the responsibility of county governments. Although traffic is often light on rural roads, the snow and ice can damage them.

CHAPTER 6

A Wealth of Goods and Services

SWEDEN HAS ONE OF THE HEALTHIEST, MOST VIBRANT economies in the world. The nation is rich in natural resources such as timber and iron ore. It is also rich in human resources. Swedish people find creative, practical solutions to economic challenges. As a result, Swedish industries have reached high levels of innovation and technology.

Exports are a key factor in Sweden's economy. Exports account for about half of Sweden's gross domestic product (GDP). That's the total value of all the country's goods and services produced in a year. In contrast, Canada's exports amount to about 31 percent of GDP and U.S. exports make up 14 percent.

Sweden's government plays a strong role in the country's economic success. It invests heavily in research and development. It also works with labor unions and businesses to assure good salaries and benefits for employees. Swedish citizens pay high taxes, but in return they enjoy a high standard of living.

Opposite: **A truck hauls logs in northern Sweden. More than 72 million cubic meters of timber were harvested in 2011.**

Cows graze in a pasture in Sweden. There are about 1.5 million cows in the country.

On the Farm

On a warm spring day, farm families and neighbors from miles around gather around the barn, their faces aglow with anticipation. At last, the barn doors swing open. Then out come the cows, trotting and leaping across the grassy trail to their pasture. After a long winter inside the barn, they are free to enjoy the sunshine, fresh air, and succulent grasses outdoors.

In many countries, dairy farmers keep their cows in indoor facilities year-round. There the cows are fed and milked, often using precisely timed, high-tech machinery. But in Sweden, dairy cows are required by law to graze outdoors at least part of the year. This stems from the belief that outdoor grazing produces happier, healthier cows and better-quality milk. Many dairy farmers oppose this law, though. They believe that indoor, mechanized dairy farming results in a higher volume of milk and more dairy income. Members of Sweden's dairy associations continue to argue on both sides of this issue.

Dairy cattle and other livestock are great sources of farm income. Besides dairy cows, farmers raise pigs, horses, sheep, chickens, and turkeys. Reindeer are the specialty among the Sámi people of northern Sweden. The dairy cows produce an abundance of milk. Other animals provide meat, and the chickens produce eggs. All these products go to Swedish markets, and many are exported to other countries.

Bountiful Crops

Livestock makes up just a part of Sweden's agricultural wealth. Sweden's farmers raise almost enough crops to feed everyone in the country. This is amazing, since Sweden has so little farmland and so few farmers. Only about 7.5 percent of the land can be used for farming, and less than 2 percent of Swedes are engaged in agriculture. Cropland in Sweden is highly productive, though.

The richest farmland is in the south, where the sunlight hours are the longest

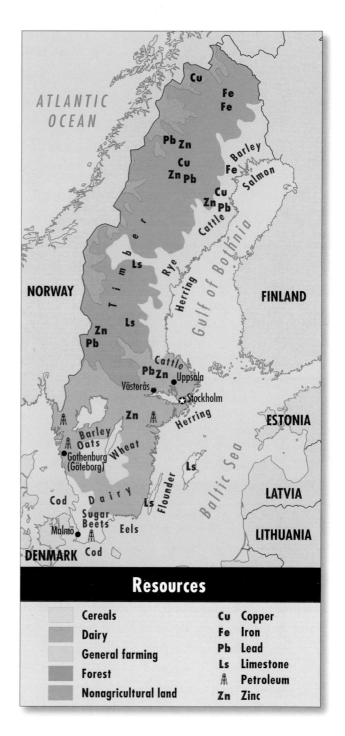

Resources

Cereals	Cu Copper
Dairy	Fe Iron
General farming	Pb Lead
Forest	Ls Limestone
Nonagricultural land	⚒ Petroleum
	Zn Zinc

and the temperatures are the warmest. Here, the growing season lasts about 240 days. Throughout the countryside in the southern province of Skåne, golden fields stretch as far as the eye can see. Many farms also thrive around the lakes in central Sweden. Even in the north, with a growing season of about 120 days, there are small tracts of land where people can grow crops.

In northern Sweden, hay and potatoes are the major crops. But farmers in the south grow a variety of products. The major crops include cereals such as wheat, barley, and oats. Other leading crops are sugar beets and vegetables. Oilseeds such as rapeseed are important, too. In the summer, southern fields are ablaze with bright-yellow rapeseed blooms. Oil from the seeds is made into canola oil and even an alternative fuel for some cars.

Money Facts

Sweden's basic unit of currency is the Swedish krona (the plural is kronor). One krona is divided into 100 öre. Banknotes, or paper bills, come in values of 20, 50, 100, 500, and 1,000 kronor, with a 200-kronor note introduced in 2015. Coins come in values of 1, 2, 5, and 10 kronor. Öre coins are no longer in use. In 2013, 1 krona equaled US$0.15 and US$1 equaled 6.62 kronor.

Each denomination of banknote is a different size, which helps people who can't see well know which bill they are spending. Each denomination is also printed in a different major color, such as purple, red, blue, or green. The front side features a famous cultural or political figure. On the back side are scenes from nature, history, or a Swedish region or city. For example, the 50-kronor note shows opera singer Jenny Lind on the front and a musical instrument called a key harp on the back.

A field of rapeseed glows in the spring sunshine. Rapeseed is used to make canola oil, a popular cooking oil in Sweden.

Forestry and Fishing

Forests cover more than half of Sweden, so forestry is big business there. Lumber and other wood products are major export goods. After being cut, the massive logs are transported by truck or railroad to sawmills for processing. Northern and north-central Sweden are the most heavily forested areas, yielding birch, pine, and spruce.

Individual people own about half the forestland in Sweden. For example, most private farms include a plot of forest trees. The rest of the forestland is evenly divided between logging companies and the government.

Strict laws regulate the harvesting of full-grown trees and the planting of new trees. This assures that forestry will remain a sustainable industry over the long term. It takes a lot of patience to comply with these laws. In southern Sweden, it can take 50 years for a newly planted pine or spruce tree to grow large enough to harvest. In the north, it can take 140 years!

Fishing is a small industry in economic terms, but it provides food for homes and restaurants, and products for exports. One major catch is herring, a popular food throughout the country. Others are cod, plaice, mackerel, and salmon. Some fishers go after shellfish such as prawns, lobsters, and crayfish. Eels are caught along the southern coasts. However, eel fisheries are strictly controlled now because the eel populations are shrinking. Gothenburg, on the west coast, is Sweden's major fishing harbor. The city's large, indoor fish market is Feskekôrka, which means "fish church." It got its name because it looks like a church.

A fisher pulls a lobster trap aboard his boat. Lobster, crab, herring, and cod are among the fish and shellfish caught in Swedish waters.

Manufacturing

Most of Sweden's exports are factory-made goods. Manufacturing accounts for about one-fifth of the country's GDP. Most factories are located along the coasts, in central Sweden, and in western Skåne.

Thanks to its rich deposits of iron ore, Sweden has a booming iron and steel industry. The nation's high-quality steel is made into everyday products such as tools and stainless steel cookware. However, Sweden's most valuable steel goods are engineering products. These include aircraft, cars, ships, farm

What Sweden Grows, Makes, and Mines

AGRICULTURE (2010)

Cow's milk	2,920,100 metric tons
Wheat	2,184,400 metric tons
Beef and pork	411,799 metric tons

MANUFACTURING

Paper and paper products (2010)	11,410,000 metric tons
Iron and crude steel (2009 est.)	6,605,555 metric tons
Automobiles (2011)	188,969 units

MINING (2009 EST.)

Iron ore	11,300,000 metric tons
Zinc ore	192,500 metric tons
Lead ore	65,000 metric tons

machinery, communications equipment, and electronics. Sweden is also the world leader in making industrial robots.

Many factories in the Bergslagen region of central Sweden produce steel, engineering equipment, and other metal products. Linköping, in south-central Sweden, is the center of the aircraft industry. Its Saab plant makes fighter jets and other high-tech aircraft. Nearby Trollhättan is the center for manufacturing Saab automobiles. This car company went bankrupt in 2012, and National Electric Vehicle Sweden (NEVS) bought the company. However, the cars are still called Saab and are still made in Trollhättan. The Volvo car company was founded in Gothenburg and is still the major employer there.

Sawmills and paper mills process Sweden's logs into lumber, wood chips, paper, and cardboard. Swedish wood is also made into furniture. The Ikea company is known for its simple, elegant furniture designs. Founded in Sweden, Ikea has hundreds of stores around the world. Food processing is another thriving industry in Sweden. Swedish chemical factories make medicines, plastics, paints, matches, and explosives. The Swedish-British pharmaceutical company AstraZeneca, founded in Sweden, has its research and development center in Södertälje.

A worker inspects microchips at Ericsson, a large technology and telecommunications company.

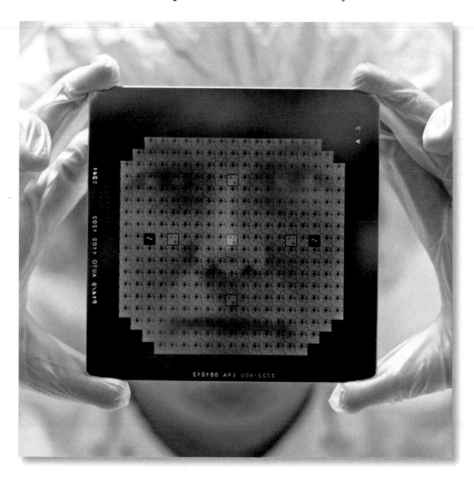

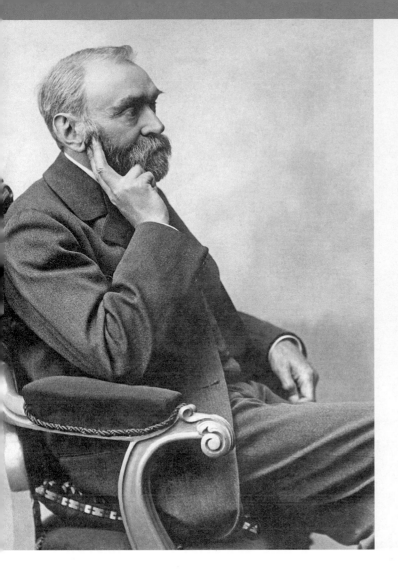

Alfred Nobel (1833–1896) was a Swedish chemist and engineer. His Bofors weapons factory made guns, cannons, and various other explosive devices. Nobel invented many types of explosives, the most famous being dynamite. He amassed a huge fortune from the sales of his inventions and weapons.

Toward the end of his life, Nobel became concerned about his contribution to society. He had been called "the merchant of death" for producing so many destructive devices, and he did not want to be remembered that way. So in his will, he left the bulk of his fortune to establish the Nobel Prizes.

Five of the six annual prizes go to people who have made significant contributions in physics, chemistry, medicine, economics, and literature. These are awarded by Swedish organizations. The sixth prize is the Nobel Peace Prize. It is awarded to someone who furthers the cause of peace and international harmony. Under the agreement made when the union between Sweden and Norway was dissolved, the Norwegian Nobel Committee gives out the peace prize. Each prizewinner receives a medal and an award of more than $1 million.

Mining

Some of the world's richest and purest deposits of iron ore are found in far-northern Kiruna. Some of this ore provides the raw material for Sweden's steel industry. However, much of it is exported.

Another mineral-rich area surrounds Skellefteå and Boliden, near the northeast coast. In fact, Skellefteå's nickname is Guldstaden, meaning "gold town." After gold was

Miners work at a drilling machine at the LKAB iron mine near Kiruna. It is the world's largest underground iron mine.

discovered near Skellefteå in 1924, the town of Boliden grew up around the gold mine. In time, this mine became one of the largest gold mines in Europe. This region is rich not only in gold, but also in copper, lead, zinc, and silver.

Service Industries

Services account for almost three-fourths of Sweden's GDP. The service industry is made up of workers who provide services instead of producing goods. More than three-fourths of Sweden's labor force is engaged in some type of service work.

City and county governments are the largest service employers. They hire health care workers such as nurses, doctors, and dentists. They also employ schoolteachers, police officers, and sanitation workers. Research scientists are service personnel, too. They help make Sweden a leader in developing innovations in biotechnology, environmentally clean technologies, and information communications technology. Other services include finance and banking, transportation, and telecommunications.

Tourism services make up a large segment of Sweden's service industry, too. Visitors use hotels and hostels, restaurants, and tour guides. They purchase clothes and souvenirs and visit museums and parks. Thousands of service workers help visitors enjoy their stay.

Transportation

In the days of the Vikings, sea travel was the best way to get around. Winter was the best time for land travel, because people could take sleds or sleighs across the frozen landscape. Transportation has changed a lot since then. A national railway system connected many cities and towns in the 1800s. Then came the automobiles.

Now highways crisscross the country, connecting cities and towns with one another and reaching into outlying areas. Major cities are connected by motorways for

Every year an ice hotel is built in the town of Jukkasjärvi, near Kiruna. The hotel and its contents, including tables, chairs, and chandeliers, are built out of snow and ice.

high-speed traffic, with speed limits of 68 or 75 miles per hour (110 or 120 kilometers per hour). The Öresund Bridge connects the southern city of Malmö with Copenhagen, Denmark.

Both passenger trains and freight trains run between major cities and into neighboring countries. Stockholm is the only city in Sweden with a rapid-transit train system. It has about one hundred stations, some underground and some aboveground. In Gothenburg, people can travel on electric trams that run down city streets and out past the city limits.

Ships are loaded with cargo at the port of Gothenburg.

Dozens of coastal cities have deep-water harbors for ships and barges. Gothenburg is the largest port city, with other major ports in Helsingborg, Malmö, and Stockholm. For air travel, Stockholm's international airport is the nation's largest. Gothenburg and Malmö also have large airports. Scandinavian Airlines System is the region's major international airline. It is jointly operated by Sweden, Denmark, and Norway.

Communications

The oldest newspaper in the world still being published is Sweden's *Post- och Inrikes Tidningar* (Post and Domestic Times). This bulletin of government news first appeared in 1645 and switched to online-only in 2007. Nevertheless, it has been produced nonstop for more than three centuries. Freedom of the press in Sweden has a long history, too. In 1766, Sweden became the first country to pass a law guaranteeing freedom of the press. This law assured that newspapers could print anything without interference from the government. The law also declared that citizens may have free access to all government documents. This level of openness is rare among the world's governments.

Today, Sweden's major daily newspapers are *Dagens Nyheter*, *Expressen*, *Svenska Dagbladet*, *Dagens Industri* (all in Stockholm), *Göteborgs-Posten* (Gothenburg), and *Sydsvenskan* (Malmö). All have both print and online editions. The *Local* offers Swedish news in the English language.

Three companies handle broadcasting in Sweden. One is in charge of several radio stations, one offers several TV channels, and the third is in charge of educational radio and

Cold Winters, Hot Ideas

Sweden is a leader in information communications technology. Two examples are the music streaming service Spotify and the video and voice service Skype. Both were invented by Swedish entrepreneurs. Daniel Ek, cofounder of Spotify, started his first company when he was fourteen years old. For Skype cofounder Niklas Zennström (right), Sweden's cold winters are the key to successful start-ups. "When the weather's like this outside," he says, "what else is there to do besides sitting inside and creating a business?"

TV. The government supervises all three to make sure their programs are objective and unbiased.

Sweden has been at the forefront of the telecommunications industry for more than a century. Back in 1876, Swedish inventor Lars Magnus Ericsson founded the telephone equipment company Ericsson. Today, Ericsson is a giant in the cell phone industry. It's the world's largest maker of wireless telecommunications equipment.

Mobile phone use is widespread in Sweden. For every one hundred Swedes, there are 119 mobile phone subscriptions. This means that thousands of Swedes have more than one mobile account. Landlines lag far behind, with forty-nine per one hundred people.

Sweden is one of the most Internet-savvy countries in the world. As of 2011, 93 percent of Swedes were Internet users. Only Iceland and Norway had higher Internet usage rates. In contrast, the U.S. usage was 78 percent and Canadian usage was 82 percent.

Computer literacy is a high priority in Sweden. The government aggressively supports broadband access throughout the country. In 1998, Sweden launched a home computing initiative (HCI). Within three years, home computer ownership almost doubled, from 41 percent of Swedish households to 80 percent. Since then, several other countries have introduced their own HCIs. Like Sweden, they recognize that computer use not only benefits individual citizens but is also good for a nation's cultural, social, and economic well-being.

A Swedish man works on his laptop in Stockholm.

CHAPTER 7

People, Language, and Learning

VAST AREAS OF SWEDEN ARE SPARSELY POPULATED. ONLY about 15 percent of the people live in rural areas. This is partly because the climate is so harsh in much of the country, making farming difficult. Jobs are easier to find in urban areas, too.

In 2013, Sweden was home to about 9.5 million people. The most densely populated regions are the Stockholm area and the southern province of Skåne. More than one-fifth of Sweden's entire population lives in Stockholm's metropolitan area, which includes the surrounding suburbs. About 13 percent of Sweden's people live in Skåne province, where the major cities are Malmö, Helsingborg, and Lund.

Immigrants and Ethnic Groups

Sweden is a haven for refugees. They are attracted to Sweden's policies of equality and openness. Immigration has increased dramatically since the late twentieth century. In 2010,

Opposite: **Swedish children race across a schoolyard. About 15 percent of the people in Sweden are under age fifteen.**

Population of Major Cities (2010 est.)

Stockholm	1,372,565
Gothenburg	549,839
Malmö	280,415
Uppsala	140,454
Västerås	110,877

about one-seventh of Sweden's population was born outside the country. The largest number of immigrants came from Finland and Iraq. The next-largest groups are from former Yugoslavian republics such as Bosnia and Herzegovina. Other immigrants came from Iran, Poland, Germany, Turkey, Denmark, and Somalia. People from many of these regions had suffered persecution, devastating wars, or both.

Ethnic Swedes continue to be the largest ethnic group in the country today. Finnish people are Sweden's largest ethnic minority. Sources differ, but between 200,000 and 470,000 ethnic Finns live in Sweden. Large communities of Finns live in Norrbotten province in northeast Sweden and in the east-central industrial city of Eskilstuna.

The Sámi

The Sámi are an indigenous ethnic group living in Sweden's Arctic region. Sámi territory spreads across the northern reaches of Norway, Sweden, Finland, and Russia. In Sweden, the Sámi population may number twenty thousand or more. Traditional Sámi ways of life include fishing along the coast, trapping fur-bearing animals, and herding sheep. But the Sámi are best known as rein-

Persons per square mile	Persons per square kilometer
more than 260	more than 100
66–260	26–100
26–65	11–25
3–25	1–10
fewer than 3	fewer than 1

deer herders. This seminomadic activity involves moving the herds from one grazing ground to another throughout the year. Only the Sámi are allowed by law to herd reindeer because it is a long-held cultural tradition.

A teacher works with a group of Iraqi teens who have recently arrived in Sweden. In 2012, about 125,000 people born in Iraq were living in Sweden.

A Somali girl at a school in Stockholm.

A Sámi family sits with its pet reindeer. The color and pattern of traditional Sámi clothing indicates where people are from.

Who Lives in Sweden?	
Swedish	83.8%
Finnish	2.9%
Former Yugoslav	2.2%
Other European	7.2%
Asian/Middle Eastern	2.4%
Other	1.5%

Much of Sámi culture has been lost over the years. Government programs banned their language, and missionaries converted the Sámi from their traditional beliefs to Lutheranism. Logging, mining, and dam building have cut into traditional Sámi territories. In time, the Sámi began to have a political voice. The Swedish government recognized the Sámi nation in 1989, and the Sámi Parliament was formed in 1993. Sámi children also gained the right to schooling in their own language. In 2011, Sweden's Supreme Court ruled that Sámi herders had the right to graze their reindeer on privately owned forestland. The court agreed that the herders' ancestors had grazed reindeer there "since time immemorial." For the Sámi, this was a major victory in reclaiming their rights.

Swedish and Other Languages

Almost two hundred languages are spoken in Sweden. This is a sign of the country's ethnic diversity. Some of the minority languages are Finnish, Arabic, Serbo-Croatian, Polish, Persian, and German. Still, most residents speak Swedish, the official national language. English is widely spoken, too. Swedish children begin learning English in elementary school.

Swedish is a Germanic language. This means it is a branch of the same language family that includes German and English. The similarity to English is sometimes obvious. For example, *moder, fader, syster, broder* means "mother, father, sister, brother." *Dörr* is "door" and *bok* is "book." Swedish is

A sign in Swedish announces that a bookshop is having a sale.

most closely related to the other Scandinavian languages, Norwegian and Danish. Swedish speakers can understand these languages to some extent, but not completely.

The Swedish government also recognizes five minority languages. This protects the cultural heritage of minority communities. The minority languages are Finnish, Sámi, Romani, Yiddish, and Meänkieli. Finnish speakers have crossed the border into Sweden for centuries. The Sámi people speak several dialects, or versions, of the Sámi language. Romani is the language of the nomadic Roma people, who originated in northern India. Yiddish is the language of Jewish people originally from central and eastern Europe. Meänkieli, related to Finnish, is spoken in the Torne Valley of northern Sweden.

A Roma girl performs a traditional dance in Stockholm. About fifty thousand Roma live in Sweden.

Common Swedish Words and Phrases

hej/hallå	hello (informal)
hej då	good-bye
tack	thanks
ja	yes
nej	no
Hur säger man . . . på svenska?	How do you say . . . in Swedish?
Vad heter du?	What is your name?
Jag heter . . .	My name is . . .

The Swedish Alphabet

Swedish people have a great sense of humor on April Fools' Day. On April 1, 2007, a Swedish newspaper made a shocking announcement: the government was thinking about getting rid of the letters *å*, *ä*, and *ö*. Keeping them was just too expensive. It was all a joke, of course.

Pronouncing Swedish

Most Swedish letters are pronounced the way an English speaker would expect. Below are a few letters pronounced differently than in English. This is only a rough guide. A native Swedish speaker is the best authority.

Letter	Pronunciation	Example
j	y as in "yes"	*hej* (hello) = "hay"
k	k as in "kite"	*kaffe* (coffee) = "kah-feh"
	sh as in "shore"	*kemin* (chemistry) = "sheh-meen"
kn	(say both letters)	*kniv* (knife) = "kuh-neev"
r	(slightly rolled)	no similar English pronunciation
å	o as in "fore"	*Skåne* (southern province) = "skoh-nuh"
ä	ai as in "hair"	*bära* (carry) = "bear-uh"
	e as in "best"	*ägg* (egg) = "egg"
ö	u as in "mud"	*röd* (red) = "rud"

The Swedish alphabet consists of twenty-nine letters. The first twenty-six are the same as those used in English, but after z come the so-called complex letters. They are $å$, $ä$, and $ö$, with capitals $Å$, $Ä$, and $Ö$. On Swedish computer keyboards, these letters are found to the right of P and L. For touch typists, the right-hand pinkie gets a good workout!

Education for All

Children of all ethnic groups, religions, income levels, and abilities have an equal right to an education in Sweden. The school year runs from the middle of August until the second week in June. Each municipality operates public preschools, primary schools, and secondary schools. Primary and secondary school tuition are free, and so are school lunches, school buses, and textbooks.

Children are required to attend nine years of school, from ages seven through sixteen. This compulsory primary school is divided into three sections. Years 1 to 3 are elementary school, years 4 to 6 are middle school, and years 7 to 9 are junior high school. Students take courses in Swedish, English, mathematics, science, social studies, religious studies, arts and crafts, physical education, and health. Religious studies include learning about all major religions. Compulsory education also includes Sámi schools, special schools, and programs for students with disabilities. Special schools are for children with hearing or vision problems or serious language problems.

After primary school comes three years of upper secondary school. Students in upper secondary school have two choices.

They may follow a vocational track to prepare for a trade, or they may pursue a college preparatory track.

Uppsala University, founded in 1477, is Sweden's oldest university. Lund, Stockholm, Gothenburg, Linköping, Umeå, and many other cities also have universities. Students may pursue any of three levels of higher education: the basic level, the advanced level, and the doctoral level. These levels are similar to bachelor's, master's, and doctoral degrees. Adult education is encouraged, too, for older people who want to improve their skills. Sweden's guarantee of equal opportunity extends to people of all ages.

Music is part of the curriculum in schools in Sweden.

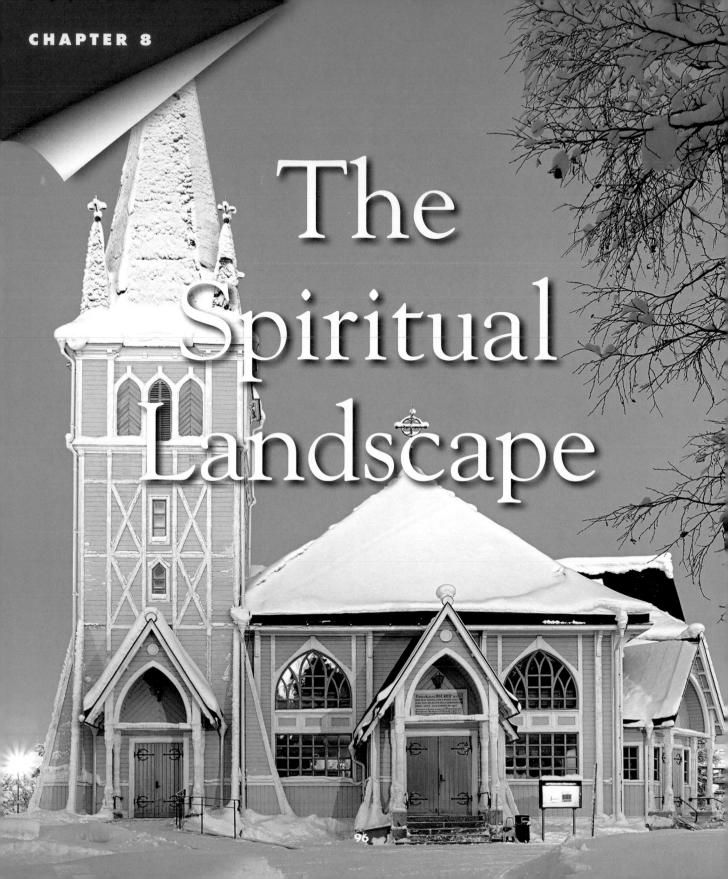

CHAPTER 8

The Spiritual Landscape

THE SWEDISH COUNTRYSIDE IS DOTTED WITH churches, many of them hundreds of years old. These churches reveal Sweden's long tradition of Christianity. For centuries, the Church of Sweden was the country's official national church. Other faiths arrived along with immigrants from many nations. Today, much of the population is secular, or nonreligious. Still, religious traditions remain in many aspects of life.

The Church of Sweden

Sweden's first Christian missionary arrived in 829. By the 1000s, Sweden had adopted Christianity. For almost five hundred years, the Roman Catholic Church was Sweden's main religion. Its leader was the pope in Rome, Italy. He appointed local church officials such as bishops and archbishops. When King Gustav I Vasa came to the throne, he insisted on appointing these officials himself. The king and the pope were in conflict on this issue until 1526, when King Gustav broke ties with the pope. He separated the Church of Sweden from the Catholic Church. (England's King Henry VIII made the same break in 1534, establishing the Church of England.)

In 1593, Swedish bishops and priests held a meeting called the Uppsala Synod. They adopted the Augsburg Confession, a declaration of the beliefs of the Lutheran faith. From that point on, the Church of Sweden was a Lutheran church. In

The Södra Råda church was built in the early 1300s. The following century, its walls were covered with extraordinary paintings. Tragically, the church burned down in 2001. Swedish officials are working on reconstructing it.

Sweden's Evangelical Lutheran Church community, the Bible holds an important place in church teachings.

For years, any child with at least one parent who belonged to the Church of Sweden automatically became a church member at birth. In 1996, a law was passed saying that only a person baptized in the church was a member. Another law in 2000 separated church and state, making the Church of Sweden no longer the official national church.

Organization and Services

The archbishop of Uppsala is the head of the Church of Sweden. Other church leaders are bishops, priests, and deacons. The country is divided into thirteen areas called dioceses, with a bishop presiding over each diocese. Bishops ordain priests and supervise church teachings. Priests oversee individual parish congregations. Priests conduct worship services, give sermons, and perform rites such as baptism. Deacons are dedicated laypeople, or parish members, who assist in church ministry.

Tuulikki Koivunen Bylund was ordained a bishop in the Church of Sweden in 2009. Currently, three of the church's thirteen bishops are women.

Since 1958, the Church of Sweden has allowed women to become priests. The first female priests were ordained in 1960. By 2008, about 35 percent of the Church of Sweden's priests were women. A woman was appointed bishop for the first time in 1997.

The main Sunday worship includes Communion, also called the Eucharist. In this ritual, the faithful receive bread and wine, which represent Jesus's body and blood. New church members are initiated through baptism, sometimes as babies, sometimes as adults. During baptism, a priest pours water over the person's forehead three times. In the confirmation ceremony, young people affirm their beliefs in the church's teachings. Often they receive their first Communion after confirmation. Priests also perform marriage and funeral ceremonies.

The Religious Calendar

Epiphany	January 6
Good Friday	Two days before Easter
Easter Sunday	March or April
Whitsunday	Fifty days after Easter
All Saints' Day	November 1
Saint Martin's Day	November 11
Advent	Four-week period before Christmas
Lucia Day	December 13
Christmas	December 25

Other Religions

Many immigrants to Sweden brought their faiths with them. Immigrants from Middle Eastern countries brought the religion of Islam. Today, Muslims, or followers of Islam, make up Sweden's second-largest religious group. An estimated half a million Muslims lived in Sweden in the early 2000s.

Muslims pray at a mosque in Stockholm. People remove their shoes when they enter a mosque.

Most of Sweden's Eastern Orthodox Christians have roots in Russia, Greece, Romania, or Serbia. About 2 percent of the population is Roman Catholic. Most are of Polish ancestry, while others came from Croatia, Bosnia and Herzegovina, or South America.

Some of Sweden's Protestants belong to so-called free churches, or nonconformist churches. These are groups that pulled away from the Church of Sweden to practice religion in their own way. They include the Mission Covenant Church of Sweden, the Pentecostal Church, and the Evangelical Free Church. Sweden is also home to members of the Jewish, Mormon, Buddhist, and Hindu faiths.

A priest performs a wedding ceremony at a Greek Orthodox church in Stockholm.

Practicing Religion

About two-thirds of Sweden's population claimed to belong to the Church of Sweden in 2012. However, a 2011 survey found that few of those members actively practice their religion. Of the 6.5 million church members, only about 400,000 attend Sunday services at least once a month. Only about 15 percent of church members said they believe in Jesus Christ. Another 15 percent claimed to be atheists, or people who do not believe in God. One-quarter of the people said they were agnostics. These are people who believe that a person cannot know whether God exists.

Some Sámi wear their traditional clothing at a church service in Jokkmokk, a town in northern Sweden.

Major Religions in Sweden (2012 est.)

Church of Sweden	6.5 million
Islam	500,000
Other Protestants	250,000
Eastern Orthodox	100,000
Roman Catholic	90,000
Others	2.5 million

This figure of Thor, one of the most powerful Norse gods, was made in about the year 1000.

Jonas Bromander, who conducted the survey, is not surprised at the results. "Many are members [of the Church of Sweden]," he says, "… because of the role the church plays in society, or because it serves as an organization which maintains Swedish traditions." In other words, people believe the church serves a useful function. For example, they support the church's social work for the poor. They also look to the church for traditions such as weddings and funerals.

Islam, too, has far fewer active members than the number of people who claim to be Muslim. For many Muslims, embracing Islam is a part of their culture rather than a regular practice of rituals.

Norse Religion

Before Christianity arrived in Scandinavia, people there followed Norse religious traditions. Norse beliefs were especially prominent during the Viking age. Much of what we know about Norse religion comes from sagas and mythic poems that tell tales of gods, kings, Viking voyages, and battles.

There were many gods in Norse religion. The major deities were Thor, Odin, and Freyr. Thor ruled the skies, commanding thunder, lightning, winds, and storms. Thor's fearsome hammer, Mjölnir, could slice through mountains with ease. Odin, Thor's father, was associated with war, magic, and wisdom. Odin's majestic hall, Valhalla, was the place where brave warriors went when they died. Freyr ruled over fertility, sunshine, and fair weather. Freyr's sister, Freyja, was a goddess of beauty and fertility. Norse legends tell of many other gods and creatures. One is Thor's mortal enemy, the Midgard Serpent. Another character is Sigurd the dragon slayer. He appears on the Ramsund rock carving in Södermanland.

Norse worship services might take place around an altar of stones, in a sacred grove of trees, or at a temple. A Norse temple once stood in the village of Gamla Uppsala, near today's Uppsala. It was said that a golden chain surrounded the temple. Housed inside were huge statues of Thor, Odin, and Freyr.

Three large burial mounds rise in Gamla Uppsala. According to ancient beliefs, they are the burial places for the three main gods. However, they are more likely the tombs of ancient kings. In the 500s CE, kings were buried at Gamla Uppsala. Before burial, the king and his armor were burned, and it was said that the leaping flames carried him to Valhalla. Many religious rituals were linked to fertility, the seasons, and the position of the sun. They were held to assure good harvests. Remnants of these ancient beliefs can still be seen in Swedish festivals today.

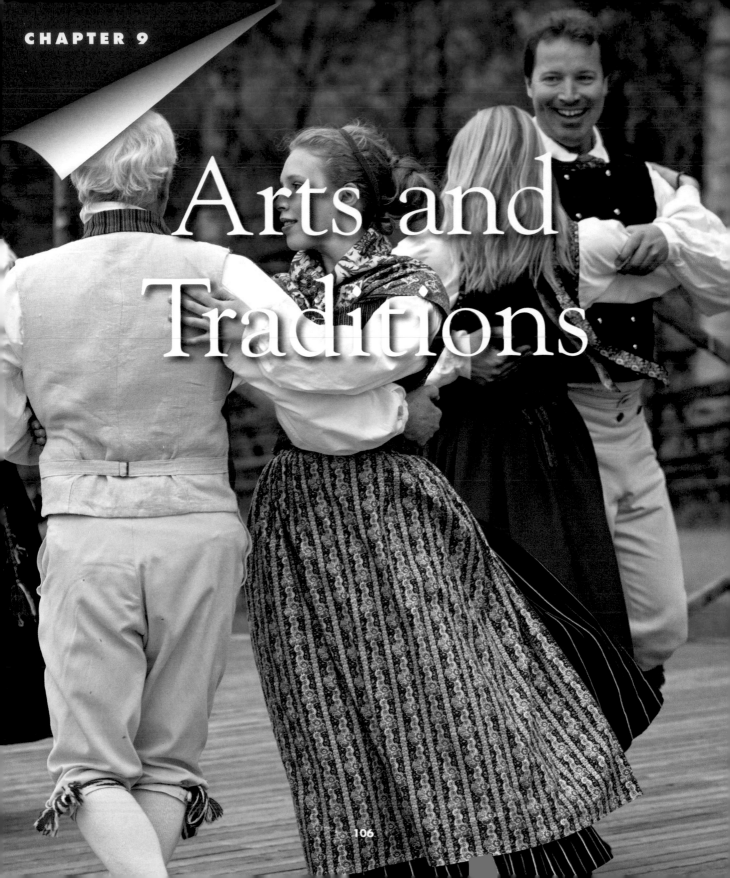

CHAPTER 9

Arts and Traditions

SWEDISH ARTS AND CULTURE HAVE ROOTS THAT reach deep into the past. Sweden's folk music traditions, for example, go back hundreds of years. Folk music accompanies dancing, with dancers decked out in regional costumes. The major instruments for folk dancing are the fiddle and the *nyckelharpa*, or key harp, a stringed instrument with keys to change the pitch. Folk music and costumed dancing died out to some extent. However, folk music lovers have revived these arts, and folk music festivals now take place all over the country. The biggest festival is held in Dalarna province in central Sweden. Dalarna has been the center of the folk music revival since the early 1900s.

On the classical music scene, Sweden's best-known composer was Franz Berwald. In the mid-1800s, he composed four symphonies and dozens of other pieces. However, audiences did not appreciate his work until the last few years of his life. In contrast, opera singer Jenny Lind was beloved all over Europe and the United States. Her nickname was the Swedish Nightingale. In the twentieth century, tenor Jussi Björling and soprano Birgit Nilsson were among the world's leading opera stars.

Opposite: **Couples dance a traditional ring dance at a midsummer celebration in Sweden.**

Sweden's biggest contribution to pop music is ABBA. The quartet constructed its name using the first letter of each member's name. In terms of record sales, ABBA is almost as popular as the Beatles. After the group won the 1974 Eurovision Song Contest, their songs topped the charts worldwide for years. Though they disbanded in 1982, ABBA still sells millions of records a year. Robyn, Swedish House Mafia, Lykke Li, and the Cardigans are some of Sweden's pop-rock stars of the early 2000s. Sweden also has its share of jazz, blues, and hip-hop artists. Both pop and classical concerts draw huge crowds.

ABBA performing in 1979. The band dominated pop music in the 1970s.

Literature

The first half of the 1800s is considered the golden age of Swedish poetry. The period saw a trend toward romanticism. One of the many poets of that time was Erik Johan Stagnelius. One of his best-known poems, "Näcken," is about a mythological water spirit, called a Nix, that entices humans into the water, where they drown.

August Strindberg was the first Swedish author to become famous outside of Sweden. His subjects show complex sides of human nature and were sometimes shocking for Swedish society at the time. For example, his play *Miss Julie* (1888) portrays a romance between an upper-class woman and a servant.

Children's books by Swedish authors are beloved worldwide. Examples are Astrid Lindgren's *Pippi Longstocking* (1945) and Selma Lagerlöf's *The Wonderful Adventures of Nils* (1906–1907). Also the author of adult novels, Lagerlöf won the Nobel Prize in Literature.

Selma Lagerlöf

In 1909, Selma Lagerlöf (1858–1940) became the first woman to receive the Nobel Prize in Literature.

Born in Värmland in the west of the country, she grew up in a mansion at Mårbacka, the family estate. While teaching at a girls' high school, she began writing her first novel, *Gösta Berlings Saga* (1891). Lagerlöf's best-known novel internationally is *The Wonderful Adventures of Nils* (1906–1907). She wrote it as a geography reader for Sweden's public schools. Nils, the hero, is a mischievous boy who flies over Sweden on the back of a goose.

Many modern Swedish crime novels have become international hits. All three books in Stieg Larsson's *Millennium* trilogy (2005–2007) have been made into movies, starting with *The Girl with the Dragon Tattoo*. Henning Mankell's detective novels feature the unconventional sleuth Kurt Wallander. Many Wallander stories have been made into movies and TV series. The stories are set in Ystad, near Malmö. Fans from around the world visit Ystad to take tours of the Wallander filming sites.

Films, Stars, and Directors

Actors Greta Garbo and Ingrid Bergman are just two of Sweden's film stars. Garbo started out in silent films in Europe before going on to fame in the United States. Ingrid Bergman is considered one of the greatest female stars of all time. Winner of three Academy Awards, she is best known for her roles in *Casablanca* (1942) and *Notorious* (1946). Other Swedish film stars include Bibi Andersson and Max von Sydow.

Many Swedish actors launched their careers in films made by director Ingmar Bergman (not related to Ingrid). He directed more than sixty films. Working with cameraman Sven Nykvist, Bergman often set his films in the haunting Swedish landscape. Common themes are religious faith, illness, insanity, and death. For example, in *The Seventh Seal* (1957), a medieval knight plays chess with Death. *In Fanny and Alexander* (1982), a brother and sister suffer under their harsh stepfather, the local bishop.

Ingrid Bergman with American actor Humphrey Bogart in a scene from *Casablanca*. Bergman was one of the great movie stars of the 1940s.

Swedish director Lasse Hallström has had great success, both in Sweden and in the United States. His films include *My Life as a Dog* (1985), *What's Eating Gilbert Grape?* (1993), *The Cider House Rules* (1999), and *Chocolat* (2000).

Art and Design

Petroglyphs, or rock carvings, were Sweden's first works of art. Many of these artworks are found in Bohuslän, on the west coast. Carved as early as 2000 BCE, they depict scenes of daily life in a coastal farming community, with human figures, religious rituals, animals, and ships.

Religious art flourished after Christianity arrived in Sweden. Albertus Pictor (Albert the Painter) adorned many churches in southern and central Sweden with wall paintings in the 1400s. Täby Church and Härkeberga Church in Uppland are just two of the dozens of churches he beautified. An Albertus painting in Täby Church depicts Death playing chess. It inspired director Ingmar Bergman's film *The Seventh Seal*.

The late 1800s ushered in a romantic art style, with subjects depicted in an ideal way. Anders Zorn painted subjects such as misty landscapes, charming peasant girls, and Swedish folk life. For Carl Larsson, his wife and eight children inspired many of his paintings of a happy home life. In the early 1900s, sculptor Carl Milles created ornate fountains and huge statues. His work includes a statue of the Greek god Poseidon displayed in Gothenburg, a statue of Gustav Vasa housed at the Nordic Museum, and statues based on the Greek story of Orpheus installed outside the Stockholm Concert Hall.

In modern times, Sweden has become famous for its industrial design. This involves combining fine arts and traditional crafts with technological know-how. The finished products are everyday objects that are beautiful, easy to use, and simple in design. Well-known examples are glassware and ceramics, Ikea furniture, Ericsson phones, and Volvo cars. More than a dozen glassworks are clustered at Glasriket (Kingdom of Crystal) in Småland. Here visitors can watch master glassmakers at work and even blow, engrave, and paint their own glass.

Visitors watch glass-blowers make a vase at a glassworks in Kosta, a city in southern Sweden that is at the heart of Sweden's glassmaking region.

CHAPTER 10

Enjoying Life

SWEDES ARE AMONG THE HAPPIEST PEOPLE IN THE world. A 2013 survey by the Organization for Economic Cooperation and Development found that Swedes ranked second only to Australians in having an overall sense of well-being and satisfaction with life. Some factors in the positive outlook of Swedes include comfortable housing, clean air and water, trust in government, job security, good health, and strong community networks.

Beyond that, however, Swedes are just plain happy. On a typical day, about six out of seven Swedes experience positive feelings of rest, enjoyment, and pride in their accomplishments.

Swedes have built a society where it's easy to enjoy life. Simple, everyday things such as housing, food, and fun offer a glimpse into this society.

Opposite: **Sweden has a long coastline. Many Swedes enjoy swimming in the sea in the summer, when the temperatures are mild.**

City and Country

Sweden's cities are modern and clean. It's easy for people to get around, either on public transportation or by car. Many residents in the cities and suburbs live in high-rise apartment buildings. As cities grew in the 1950s and 1960s, the government built thousands of new housing units. By the early 2000s, more than half of Swedish households called apartments home. The rest lived in individual houses. Many cities have older sections, where houses with red-tiled roofs and flower boxes line cobblestone streets.

Colorful balconies decorate this apartment building in Stockholm.

Throughout the Swedish countryside there are red cottages everywhere. Red has been a popular house color for hundreds of years. Some people who live in rural areas are farmers. Others have city jobs but prefer the peace and quiet of rural life. Some rural residents split their time between farmwork and factory work.

Eating in Sweden

Swedish people enjoy a wealth of fresh foods. Fish and shellfish, fruits and berries, mushrooms, vegetables, wild game, and farm animals are all available locally. These are blended into delicious traditional dishes. All cooks have their favorite recipe for *köttbullar*, or Swedish meatballs. They're considered

the national dish. The meatballs are usually served with side dishes of mashed or boiled potatoes and lingonberries.

Any festive meal can be a *smörgåsbord*. This is an array of cold and hot dishes spread out on a table. Smörgåsbords include cold fish such as salmon, shrimp, and pickled herring; cold, sliced meats such as ham and reindeer; and hot meatballs, herring, and sausages. A smörgåsbord might have as many as a hundred different foods!

A warm August night is the perfect time for a crayfish supper. It's held outdoors with colored paper lanterns strung around the picnic area. The crayfish, small relatives of lobsters, are boiled in a big pot of salt water seasoned with dill. Guests wear bibs and cone-shaped hats. Thursday is the day when people like to eat yellow pea soup with pork, followed by thin pancakes. This custom comes from pre-Lutheran times when Friday was a day for fasting.

Only the hardiest foodies can bear to eat *surströmming*, or sour herring. This consists of small Baltic herring fermented in salt water. They are packed in tins that swell as the fermenting process continues. When the tin is opened, out bursts

Let's Make Swedish Meatballs!

Swedish meatballs, or *köttbullar*, are must-haves for any Swedish feast. Make sure an adult is around to help you make this dish. This recipe makes four to six servings.

Ingredients

1 medium onion

Butter

¾ cup dry bread crumbs

1 cup milk

1.5 pounds ground beef or mixed ground beef and pork

1 large egg

Salt

White pepper

Allspice

Directions

Chop the onion finely. Melt about 2 tablespoons of butter in a skillet, and sauté the onion in it for about 2 minutes, until it's soft. In a small bowl, soak the bread crumbs in the milk. Once the bread is soaked, squeeze out the extra milk. Put the ground meat in a large bowl. Add the bread crumbs and egg. Sprinkle with some salt, pepper, and allspice. Mix well, using your hands if you don't mind the mess. Form the mixture into 1-inch balls, using your hands or two tablespoons. Melt about 2 or 3 tablespoons of butter in a large skillet and place the meatballs in it. Shake and stir the skillet until the meatballs are brown on all sides and cooked through the center. Enjoy!

an overwhelming odor of rotting fish. The odor alone makes some people sick, but surströmming fans love it. The fish are traditionally served with a crispy flatbread, often with potatoes and chopped onions to offset the sour taste.

More Food Traditions

Special occasions like birthdays call for a princess cake. It's covered with green marzipan, a sugary almond paste, and topped with a pink marzipan rose.

It's hard to name all of Sweden's traditional foods. Any list would include wild lingonberries fresh from the forest. They are preserved as jam or made into a sauce for pancakes. *Knäckebröd*, or crisp bread, is popular for eating with cheese or meat slices, or just butter. Shrimp sandwiches are a favorite choice, too. Like many sandwiches in Sweden, they're served open-face, on one piece of bread.

Finally, no day is complete without at least one *fika* (pronounced FEE-kah). A fika is something like a coffee break. It's a chance for friends to meet, talk over their day, and enjoy a beverage and pastries. Adults and teenagers alike can sit for hours at a café enjoying this time-honored Swedish tradition.

Celebrating the Seasons

Swedes wait so long for warm weather, it's no wonder they have special festivals to celebrate spring and summer. Spring weather comes at different times in different parts of the country. Still, everyone welcomes the coming of spring with the Feast of Valborg on April 30.

Playing the Viking Game

Both children and adults enjoy playing *kubb* (pronounced KOOB). It's also called the Viking game. Supposedly, kubb originated among the Vikings on Gotland Island, but no one has ever proved this. It's played outdoors on a rectangular court, with two teams. One person or a group of people can make up a team.

The two teams face each other on opposite sides of the court. Five kubbs, or wooden blocks, are lined up along each team's baseline. In the center of the court is the tall wooden king. Team members throw wooden sticks at the other team's kubbs, trying to knock them down.

Once one team knocks down all the other side's kubbs, team members can go for the king. When they knock down the king, they win the game. However, if anyone knocks the king down before the other kubbs are down, that person's side loses instantly.

On this day, all over Sweden people light huge bonfires, piling on any old household junk to make the fire blaze higher. In the warm glow of the fire, they drink hot cocoa and munch hot dogs. Singing in choirs is popular in Sweden, and Valborg brings out choirs singing spring songs around the bonfires. Students in university towns such as Uppsala and Lund hold huge, all-day celebrations for Valborg. Thousands of spectators come to watch Uppsala students raft down the Fyris River in wildly inventive rafts.

People all over the country celebrate Midsummer's Eve around June 21. That is the time of the summer solstice, the longest day of the year. Many ancient folk traditions surround Midsummer's Eve. People believed the night was filled with supernatural happenings, with magic lurking everywhere. Today, people decorate their homes, cars, and villages with garlands of flowers. Then they gather on the town square or a playground to raise the maypole. This is a tall cross, bedecked with leaves and flowers. Dancers grab a partner and dance round and round the maypole. The dancing continues outdoors or in a barn that night. Typical Midsummer's Eve food is pickled herring, new potatoes with dill, and a strawberry dessert.

Public Holidays

New Year's Day	January 1
Epiphany	January 6
Good Friday	Late March/early April
Easter Sunday	Late March/early April
Easter Monday	Day after Easter
May Day	May 1
Ascension Day (40 days after Easter)	Date varies
Whitsunday (7th Sunday after Easter)	Date varies
National Day	June 6
Midsummer's Day	Saturday during June 20–26
All Saints' Day	Saturday during Oct. 30–Nov. 6
Christmas	December 25
Boxing Day	December 26

Note: The day before an official holiday is often treated as a holiday, too. Examples are Valborg, Midsummer's Eve, Christmas Eve, and New Year's Eve. Most businesses are closed on those days.

Large family gatherings are often held on the Midsummer holiday. Everyone dances around the maypole and enjoys the good company.

Religious Holiday Traditions

Devout church members attend church services on religious holidays. However, even the most secular people celebrate these holidays in their own way. The four weeks before Christmas make up the season of Advent. One Advent custom is to light a candle on each of the four Sundays of Advent. Another custom is to hang a star in the window during these weeks. It symbolizes the star that the Three Wise Men followed to Jesus's birthplace. Children enjoy the countdown to Christmas on an Advent calendar. Each day on the calendar has a window that opens up to reveal a picture, a poem, or a small gift. Friends also get together for *glögg* (hot, sugared wine) and gingerbread during this time.

Getting Married

Some Swedish couples hold their wedding in a park or at the seashore, and even though religious devotion is dwindling, many Swedish couples hold their wedding in a church. The bride and groom walk down the church aisle together, each with one attendant. A popular joke is that whoever says "I do" the loudest will be the head of the household!

Traditionally, the bride wore a crown of myrtle leaves as a sign of innocence. Today, brides are more likely to wear a tiara. Brides traditionally wear three rings on their wedding day—one for the engagement, one for the wedding, and one for motherhood.

A reception follows the ceremony, with a smörgåsbord or buffet dinner and wedding cake. People sing traditional wedding songs, and anyone is welcome to make a speech, so the celebration can go on for hours.

Lucia Day, December 13, has a mixture of origins. The celebration partly honors Saint Lucia and partly draws on ancient rural customs. Today, a girl is chosen as Lucia. She leads a nighttime procession wearing a white robe and red sash. On her head is a wreath of lightbulbs. Behind Lucia are her handmaidens carrying one candle each, and star boys carrying large golden stars and wearing white wizard hats decorated with stars. Lucia

processions take place all over Sweden. Besides the national
Lucia, there is a Lucia in every town and many schools, too.
The Lucias visit malls and elderly people's homes, often passing
out gingersnaps and saffron-flavored Saint Lucia buns.

The Yule goat is a familiar ornament at Christmastime. It's
usually made of straw with a red ribbon tied around it. Yule
goats have a long history in Swedish folklore. They stood for
the end of the harvest, the spirit of mischief, or the giver of
gifts. Some towns place a giant Yule goat in the town square.
The most famous of these is the Gävle Goat, in Gävle.

Most people celebrate Christmas on Christmas Eve. Many
families begin at 3:00 p.m. by watching movies on TV. Then
relatives and friends get together to eat and to exchange
gifts. Christmas dinner includes a lavish spread of traditional

foods, such as pickled herring, boiled potatoes, pork sausages, a Christmas ham with mustard, a fish dish called *lutfisk*, and rice pudding. At one point, the doorbell rings and in comes *Jultomten* (Santa Claus) to hand out children's gifts. Some children can't help wondering: Why is Pappa never around when Jultomten comes?

Easter traditions include painting Easter eggs and decorating the house. Typical decorations arc willow and birch twigs, bunches of colored feathers, and figures of chickens, rabbits,

The town of Gävle has been building a giant goat from straw every Christmas season since the 1960s. This goat is more than 40 feet (12 m) tall.

and witches. On the Thursday before Easter, children dress up as Easter witches with ragged skirts and painted cheeks. They go door-to-door asking for treats. This comes from a folklore belief that witches flew to a place called Blåkulla (blue hill) to meet the devil that day. Again, Christianity and ancient beliefs mix together in Sweden's unique culture.

Sports and Recreation

Swedish athletes excel at ice hockey, soccer, skiing, tennis, and golf. Millions of fans watch soccer and ice hockey games on TV. The country's biggest sports star is Zlatan Ibrahimović, the captain of Sweden's national soccer team. Tennis champion Björn Borg won dozens of international titles in the 1970s. He is considered one of the greatest tennis players of all time.

Most people in Sweden take part in some kind of outdoor activity. In the spring and summer, nature lovers head for the

Soccer Star

Zlatan Ibrahimović was born in Malmö in 1981 to immigrants from Bosnia and Croatia. The family lived in Malmö's Rosengård neighborhood, home to many immigrants. Zlatan began playing soccer when he was six. He signed on to Malmö's top-notch team in his teens and then moved on to playing for teams in other countries. Meanwhile, he joined Sweden's national team in 2001 and became captain in 2010. Ibrahimović never forgot his childhood home. In 2007, he donated a new soccer field to the Rosengård district. The field is located in the same spot where he used to play as a child.

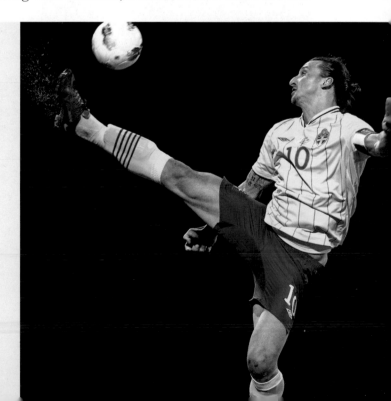

A man barbecues on an island in the Stockholm Archipelago. The islands are a favorite place for Swedes to spend beautiful summer days.

forests to pick wildflowers, wild berries, and mushrooms. The Swedish constitution guarantees the "right to roam." That means people may walk, cycle, ski, swim, or camp on any private, nonfarm land as long as they don't damage it. Bicycling is both a form of recreation and a way to get from place to place. It's common to take bike paths around town or cycle out into the countryside. Sweden's rushing rivers are great for fishing, canoeing, kayaking, and rafting. The many lakes and long coastline lure boaters and fishers, too.

In the winter, people enjoy snowmobiling, ice-skating, hockey, and cross-country and downhill skiing. When schools close for a week in February, many families take a ski vacation in the north. Golfers can play under the midnight sun at Björkliden Arctic Golf Course in Kiruna. It's the world's northernmost golf course. A special rule applies there: If a reindeer moves a player's golf ball, he or she gets to move it back without a penalty!

Timeline

SWEDISH HISTORY		WORLD HISTORY	
A village at Segebro becomes Sweden's earliest known settlement.	ca. 9000 BCE		
Farming is established in what is now Sweden.	ca. 2500 BCE	ca. 2500 BCE	The Egyptians build the pyramids and the Sphinx in Giza.
		ca. 563 BCE	The Buddha is born in India.
		313 CE	The Roman emperor Constantine legalizes Christianity.
		610	The Prophet Muhammad begins preaching a new religion called Islam.
Sweden's Vikings trade with and attack neighboring lands.	ca. 700s-1000s CE		
A monk named Ansgar brings Christianity to Sweden.	829		
King Olof Skötkonung accepts Christianity.	ca. 1000		
		1054	The Eastern (Orthodox) and Western (Roman Catholic) Churches break apart.
		1095	The Crusades begin.
		1215	King John seals the Magna Carta.
		1300s	The Renaissance begins in Italy.
		1347	The plague sweeps through Europe.
Norway, Sweden, and Denmark join together in the Kalmar Union.	1397	1453	Ottoman Turks capture Constantinople, conquering the Byzantine Empire.
		1492	Columbus arrives in North America.
Lutheranism becomes Sweden's official religion.	1500s	1500s	Reformers break away from the Catholic Church, and Protestantism is born.
Gustav Vasa becomes king, and Sweden gains independence.	1523		
The Swedish Empire comes to an end.	1721		
		1776	The U.S. Declaration of Independence is signed.

SWEDISH HISTORY

Sweden loses Finland to Russia; Sweden adopts a new constitution.	**1809**
Sweden gains Norway from Denmark.	**1814**
Large numbers of Swedes start to leave the country.	**mid-1800s**
Norway separates from Sweden.	**1905**
Sweden remains neutral during World War I.	**1914–1918**
Sweden remains neutral during World War II.	**1939–1945**
Sweden joins the United Nations.	**1946**
Sweden's Dag Hammarskjöld is elected UN secretary-general.	**1953**
Sweden's new constitution reduces the power of the king.	**1974**
Sweden joins the European Union.	**1995**
Sweden declares separation of church and state.	**2000**
Swedish voters reject the euro.	**2003**
Fredrik Reinfeldt becomes prime minister.	**2006**
Reinfeldt is elected to a second term.	**2010**

WORLD HISTORY

1789	The French Revolution begins.
1865	The American Civil War ends.
1879	The first practical lightbulb is invented.
1914	World War I begins.
1917	The Bolshevik Revolution brings communism to Russia.
1929	A worldwide economic depression begins.
1939	World War II begins.
1945	World War II ends.
1969	Humans land on the Moon.
1975	The Vietnam War ends.
1989	The Berlin Wall is torn down as communism crumbles in Eastern Europe.
1991	The Soviet Union breaks into separate states.
2001	Terrorists attack the World Trade Center in New York City and the Pentagon near Washington, D.C.
2004	A tsunami in the Indian Ocean destroys coastlines in Africa, India, and Southeast Asia.
2008	The United States elects its first African American president.

Fast Facts

Official name: Kingdom of Sweden

Capital: Stockholm

Official language: Swedish

Gothenburg

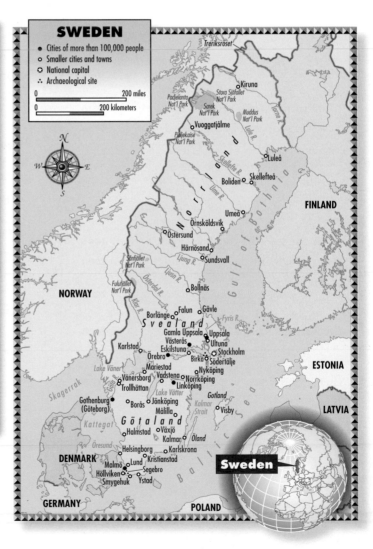

SWEDEN
- Cities of more than 100,000 people
- Smaller cities and towns
- National capital
- Archaeological site

0   200 miles
0   200 kilometers

Treriksröset

Kiruna

Stora Sjöfallet Nat'l Park
Padjelanta Nat'l Park
Sarek Nat'l Park
Muddus Nat'l Park
Vuoggatjälme
Padjekaise Nat'l Park
Boliden
Skellefteå
Luleå

Umeå
Örnsköldsvik
Östersund
Härnösand
Sundsvall
Sånfjället Nat'l Park
Ljung R.
Ljusn R.
Fulufjäller Nat'l Park
Österdal R.
Bollnäs
Falun
Gävle
Borlänge
Svealand
Fyris R.
Gamla Uppsala
Uppsala
Västerås
Ultuna
Karlstad
Eskilstuna
Stockholm
Örebro
Birka
Södertälje
Mariestad
Nyköping
Lake Väner
Vadstena
Norrköping
Vänersborg
Linköping
Trollhättan
Lake Vätter
Gotland
Gothenburg (Göteborg)
Jönköping
Borås
Målilla
Kalmar Strait
Visby
Götaland
Kattegat
Växjö
Halmstad
Kalmar
Öland
Öresund
Helsingborg
Karlskrona
Lund
Kristianstad
Malmö
Segebro
Höllviken
Smygehuk
Ystad

Norrland
Skellefte R.
Ume R.
Lule R.
Torne R.
Gulf of Bothnia
Baltic Sea
Skagerrak

NORWAY
FINLAND
ESTONIA
LATVIA
DENMARK
GERMANY
POLAND

Sweden

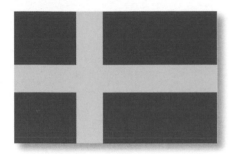

Swedish flag

Official religion: None

National anthem: "Du Gamla, Du Fria" ("Thou Ancient, Thou Free")

Type of government: Constitutional monarchy

Head of state: King

Head of government: Prime minister

Area: 173,860 square miles (450,295 sq km)

Latitude and longitude of geographic center: 62°23'15" N, 16°19'32" E

Bordering countries: Norway to the west, Finland to the northeast

Highest elevation: Mount Kebnekaise, 6,926 feet (2,111 m) above sea level

Lowest elevation: Lake Hammarsjö, 7.9 feet (2.4 m) below sea level

Coastline: 2,200 miles (3,540 km) long

Average daily high temperature: In Stockholm, 31°F (–1°C) in January, 72°F (22°C) in July; in Kiruna, 12°F (–11°C) in January, 64°F (18°C) in July

Average daily low temperature: In Stockholm, 23°F (–5°C) in January, 56°F (13°C) in July; in Kiruna, –6°F (–21°C) in January, 45°F (7°C) in July

Average annual precipitation: 24 inches (61 cm)

Sarek National Park

Öresund Bridge

Currency

National population (2013 est.):	9,566,945	

Population of major cities (2010 est.):	Stockholm	1,372,565
	Gothenburg	549,839
	Malmö	280,415
	Uppsala	140,454
	Västerås	110,877

Landmarks:
- ▶ *Gamla Stan*, Stockholm
- ▶ *Modern Museum*, Malmö
- ▶ *Öresund Bridge*, Malmö
- ▶ *Stockholm Archipelago*, offshore Stockholm
- ▶ *Uppsala Cathedral*, Uppsala

Economy: Sweden is rich in timber, iron ore, and hydroelectric power. The nation's economy depends heavily on its exports. Its major industries center on forestry, telecommunications, automotive goods, and pharmaceutical products. Important agricultural products include milk, wheat, beef, and barley.

Currency: The Swedish krona. In 2013, 1 krona equaled US$0.15 and US$1 equaled 6.62 kronor.

System of weights and measures: Metric system

Literacy rate (2012): 99%

Students

Carl Linnaeus

Common Swedish words and phrases:

hej/hallå	hello (informal)
hej då	good-bye
tack	thanks
ja	yes
nej	no
Hur säger man…på svenska?	How do you say…in Swedish?
Vad heter du?	What is your name?
Jag heter…	My name is…

Prominent Swedes:

Ingmar Bergman (1918–2007)
Film director

Ingrid Bergman (1915–1982)
Actor

Dag Hammarskjöld (1905–1961)
Diplomat

Selma Lagerlöf (1858–1940)
Writer

Astrid Lindgren (1907–2002)
Writer

Carl Linnaeus (1707–1778)
Scientist

Alfred Nobel (1833–1896)
Chemist

August Strindberg (1849–1912)
Playwright

Raoul Wallenberg (1912–ca. 1947)
Diplomat and humanitarian

To Find Out More

Books

- Anderson, Margaret J. *Carl Linnaeus: Father of Classification.* Berkeley Heights, NJ: Enslow Publishers, 2009.

- Borden, Louise W. *His Name Was Raoul Wallenberg.* Boston: Houghton Mifflin, 2012.

- Margeson, Susan. *Viking.* New York: Dorling Kindersley, 2010.

- Wargin, Kathy-Jo. *Alfred Nobel: The Man Behind the Peace Prize.* Chelsea, MI: Sleeping Bear Press, 2009.

DVDs

- *Cities of the World: Sweden.* Shepherd Entertainment, 2011.

- *Families of Sweden.* Master Communications, 2010.

- *Sweden: My House in Sweden.* New Dimension Media, 2011.

▶ Visit this Scholastic Web site for more information on Sweden:
www.factsfornow.scholastic.com
Enter the keyword **Sweden**

Index

Page numbers in *italics*
indicate illustrations.

Meet the Author

ANN HEINRICHS BEGINS TO GET ITCHY IF SHE HASN'T been out of the country for a while. She has traveled through much of Europe, as well as the Middle East, East Asia, and Africa. Writing about other countries and cultures keeps her in touch with places she's visited and those she hopes to visit someday.

Heinrichs grew up roaming the woods of Arkansas. Now she lives in Chicago's Swedish neighborhood of Andersonville, where she's a frequent customer at the Swedish Bakery. She has written more than two hundred books for children and young adults on American, European, Asian, and African history and culture. Some of her other titles in the Enchantment of the World series are *Brazil*, *Japan*, *Egypt*, *Niger*, *Nigeria*, *Ethiopia*, and *Wales*. Several of her books have won state and national awards.

"When I'm starting a country book," says Heinrichs, "I head for the library's reference department. Some of my must-see resources are *Europa World Year Book* and the periodicals databases. For this book, I also read online issues of *Nordstjernan*, the *Local*, and other newspapers to get a feel for Swedes' current interests and viewpoints. The Swedish government's statistics Web site was very helpful, and so were United Nations sites such as UNESCO, UNICEF, and the Human Development Reports."

Heinrichs prefers writing nonfiction to fiction. "I guess I'm a frustrated journalist," she says. "I'm driven to track down facts and present them in an engaging way. For me, facts are more exciting than fiction, and I want my readers to experience a subject as passionately as I do. Also, I feel it's vital for American kids to understand unfamiliar cultures, so I like to report on what kids in another country are up to—their interests, values, and daily lives, as well as their economic role in the family."

Heinrichs has also written numerous newspaper, magazine, and encyclopedia articles. As an advertising copywriter, she has covered everything from plumbing hardware to Oriental rugs. She holds bachelor's and master's degrees in piano performance and, most recently, a master of library and information science degree. For fun, she enjoys bicycling along Chicago's lakefront and kayaking.

Photo Credits